Men Are Like Waffles— Women Are Like Spaghetti

Bill and Pam Farrel

HARVEST HOUSE PUBLISHERS

EUGENE, OREGON

Cover by Left Coast Design, Portland, Oregon

Published in association with the literary agency of Alive Communications, Inc., 7680 Goddard
Street, Ste #200, Colorado Springs, CO 80920

MEN ARE LIKE WAFFLES—WOMEN ARE LIKE SPAGHETTI

Copyright © 2001 by Bill and Pam Farrel
Published by Harvest House Publishers
Eugene, Oregon 97402
www.harvesthousepublishers.com

The Library of Congress has cataloged the edition as follows:
ISBN 978-0-7369-1961-6

Library of Congress Cataloging-in-Publication Data
Farrel, Bill, 1959–
    Men are like waffles, women are like spaghetti / Bill and Pam Farrel.
        p. cm.
    ISBN 0-7369-0486-7
        1. Man-woman relationships.   2. Interpersonal communications.   3. Interpersonal rela-
    tions.   I. Farrel, Pam, 1959–   II. Title.
HQ801.F353 2001
306.7—dc21   00-047127

Printed in the United States of America

11   12   13   14   15 / LB / 15   14   13   12   11

*To the faithful supporters of Masterful Living Ministries
for believing the message behind*
Men Are like Waffles—Women Are like Spaghetti
will build and encourage marriages.

Contents

So God created man in his own image,
in the image of God he created him;
male and female he created them.

—Genesis 1:27

Accept one another, then,
just as Christ accepted you,
in order to bring praise to God.

—Romans 15:7

What's the Difference?

We Need to See I to I

"There are two types of people in this world—those who categorize people into one of two groups and those who do not." [1]

At the very beginning of history God said, "Let us make man in our image, in our likeness...So God created man in his own image, in the image of God he created him; male and female he created them" (Genesis 1:26-27).

It was in God's plan to make us different from each other from the moment he imagined us. The original plan was to use these differences as a starting point for building intimate, fulfilling relationships. Unfortunately, what started out as an advantage has turned out to be a universal source of frustration. Because we are all experientially familiar with the turmoil of relationships, we easily laugh at stories such as these:

Mel's son rushed in the door. "Dad! Dad!" he announced. "I got a part in the school play!"

"That's terrific," Mel said proudly. "What part is it?"

"I play the part of the dad."

Mel thought this over. "Go back tomorrow," he instructed, "and tell them you want a speaking role."[2]

While we were vacationing at Bryce Canyon National Park in Utah, our motor home began acting up. I had become a "bear" trying to fix all the problems. My wife, Diane, was hardly speaking to me by the time we went to the park's general store for groceries. She picked up a bag of ice. "I'll take this," she said to the clerk. "It's the warmest thing I've had my arms around all day."[3]

Despite the frustration, the vast majority of us have an undeniable desire to have great relationships with the opposite sex. We want both male and female friends, we want successful business relationships with both men and women, and we want marriages that are happy and harmonious. That is why so many of our decisions are affected by how the opposite sex will respond.

I accompanied Bill to a lawn-equipment store to look at used riding mowers. After examining the array, Bill wanted to "think about it." Not wanting to lose a sale, the sales manager quickly mentioned their 60-day, no-interest payment program.

"Sounds great," Bill said, "but I have to talk this over with my wife or there'll be 60-days, no-interest at home."[4]

It is possible to make too much out of the differences between men and women, but it is also possible to make the opposite mistake. If you want to have relationships that add to your life rather than make you exhausted, it seems to us that the place to start is with an understanding of the uniqueness each gender brings to the relationship.

Dive into the Differences

So, how are you to understand the differences between men and women? We like to think of them this way: Men are like waffles, women are like spaghetti. At first this may seem silly, even juvenile, but stay with us. It is a picture that works and men "get it" (because it involves food).

Men Are like Waffles

We do not mean that men "waffle" on all decisions and are generally unstable. What we mean is that men process life in boxes. If you look down at a waffle, you see a collection of boxes separated by walls. The boxes are all separate from each other and make convenient holding places. That is typically how a man processes life. Our thinking is divided up into boxes that have room for one issue and one issue only. The first issue of life goes in the first box, the second goes in the second box, and so on. The typical man lives in one box at a time and one box only. When a man is at work, he is at work. When he is in the garage tinkering around, he is in the garage tinkering. When he is watching TV, he is simply watching TV. That is why he looks as though he is in a trance and can ignore everything else going on around him. Social scientists call this "compartmentalizing"—that is, putting life and responsibilities into different compartments.

As a result, men are problem solvers by nature. They enter a box, size up the "problem," and formulate a solution. In their careers, they consider what it will take to be successful and focus on it. In communication, they look for the bottom line and get there as quickly as possible. In decision-making, they look for an approach they can buy into and apply it as often as possible.

A man will strategically organize his life in boxes and then spend most of his time in the boxes *he can succeed in*. This is such a strong motivation for him that he will seek out the boxes that work and will ignore the boxes that confuse him or make him feel like a failure. For instance, a man whose career holds the possibility of success will spend more and more time at work at the expense of other priorities. On the other hand, a man who always falls short at work or feels he never meets the expectations around him may find out that he is pretty good at being lazy. He will then develop a commitment to being lazy because he knows he can do that today with the same proficiency as yesterday.

Men also take a "success" approach to communication. If they believe they can successfully talk with their wives and reach a desirable outcome, they will be highly motivated to converse. If, on the other hand, the conversation seems pointless to him or he finds understanding his wife impossible, he loses his motivation to talk and clams up. That is why men come up with profound things to say, such as, "Is there any point to this conversation? Is this conversation leading anywhere? Can you just get to the point?" These are statements a man makes out of frustration because he doesn't know how to make conversation with his wife work.

The "success" drive is why men find it so easy to develop hobbies that consume their time. If a man finds something he is good at, it makes him feel good about himself and about his life. Because men tend to be good with mechanical and spatial activities, they get emotionally attached to building, fixing, and chasing things. Yard projects become expressions of his personality. The car becomes his signature. Fishing becomes an all-consuming pursuit of the right equipment, the right fishing spot, and the right friends. The computer stops being a tool of work as it transforms into an educational, entertaining, even intimate friend. It makes predictable moves and gives predictable feedback. Because a man knows what he will get back from his computer, he spends more and more time with this keyboard while he spends less and less time face to face with his wife.

The bottom line with men is: they feel best about themselves when they are solving problems. Therefore, they spend most of their time doing what they are best at while they attempt to ignore the things which cause them to feel deficient.

Women Are like Spaghetti

In contrast to men's waffle-like approach, women process life more like a plate of pasta. If you look at a plate of spaghetti, you notice that there are lots of individual noodles that all touch one another. If you attempted to follow one noodle around the plate, you would intersect a lot of other noodles, and you might even switch to another noodle seamlessly. That is how women face life. Every thought and issue is connected to every other thought and issue in some way. Life is much more of a process for women than it is for men.

This is why women are typically better at multitasking than men. She can talk on the phone, prepare a meal, make a shopping list, work on the agenda for tomorrow's business meeting, give instructions to her children as they are going out to play, and close the door with her foot without skipping a beat. Because all her thoughts, emotions, and convictions are connected, she is able to process more information and keep track of more activities.

As a result, most women are in pursuit of connecting life together. They solve problems but from a much different perspective than men. For women to quickly solve a problem when the issues involved in the discussion are disconnected from each other is an act of denial. And so women consistently sense the need to talk things through. In conversation she can link together the logical, emotional, relational, and spiritual aspects of the issue. The links come to her naturally so the conversation is effortless for her. If she is able to connect all the issues together, the answer to the question at hand bubbles to the surface and is readily accepted.

This often creates significant stress for couples because while she is making all the connections, he is frantically jumping boxes trying to keep up with the conversation. The man's eyes are rolling back in his head while a tidal wave of information is swallowing him up. When she is done, she feels better and he is overwhelmed. The conversation might look something like this:

Joan gets home and says, "Honey, how was your day? I had a good day today. We just committed to a new educational wing at the university, and I have been asked to oversee the budget. I am so excited that they didn't rule me out because I am a woman. You know women have been fighting for a place in society for decades, and it is good to see so much progress being made. I think it is neat that you treat the women who work for you with so much respect. Our daughter is so lucky to have you for a dad. Did you remember that Susie has a soccer game tonight? I think it is important we are there because the Johnsons are going to be there, and I really want you to meet them. Susie and Bethany are getting to be good friends, and I think we should get to know her parents as well."

As Joan is exploring this conversation, Dan is getting lost. He has no idea what the budget at the university has to do with their daughter's soccer game and their need to have a friendship with the Johnsons. He admires her ability to connect seemingly unrelated thoughts but he just can't seem to understand how she does it.

One of the characteristics that creates havoc in male/female interaction is the fact that most men have boxes in their waffle that have no words. There are thoughts in these boxes about the past, their work, and pleasant experiences, but these thoughts do not turn into words. A man is able to be quite happy in these wordless boxes because the memories he carries in them have significant meaning to him. The problem is that he cannot communicate these experiences to others, and so his wife may feel left out.

Not all of the wordless boxes have thoughts, however. There are actually boxes in the average man's waffle that contain no words and no thoughts. These boxes are just as blank as a white sheet of paper. They are EMPTY! To help relieve stress in his life, he will "park" in these boxes to relax. Amazingly, his wife always seems to notice when he is in park. She observes his blank look and the relaxed posture he has taken on the couch. She assumes this is a good time to talk as he is so relaxed, and so she invariably asks, "What are you thinking, sweetheart?"

He immediately panics because he knows if he tells the truth, she will think he is lying. She cannot imagine a moment without words in her mind. If he says, "Nothing," she thinks he is hiding something and is afraid to talk about it. She becomes instantly curious and mildly suspicious. Not wanting to disappoint his wife, his eyes start darting back and forth hoping to find some box in close proximity that has words in it. If he finds a box of words quickly he will engage his wife in conversation and both will feel good about the relationship. If he is slow in finding words, her suspicion fails to be extinguished, and he feels a sense of failure. He desperately wants to explain to his wife that he sometimes just goes blank. Nothing is wrong, nothing is in denial, and nothing is being hidden. This is the way he has been his whole life, but she cannot imagine it.

These blank boxes have an interesting characteristic that often gets in the way of meaningful conversation. In the middle of conversation a man will periodically be moving from one box to another, and in between two boxes of words he passes through one of these blank boxes. Right in the middle of conversation, he goes silent. He knows he should have something to say, but he is blank. He knows it is awkward to go blank in the middle of a thought, but no amount of effort has ever made it go away. It is an awkwardness he must live with and hope his wife adapts to.

Different by Design

The differences are not limited to conversation, however. As research accumulates, it is becoming increasingly obvious that God made men and women different in many ways. They think differently, they process emotions differently, they make decisions differently, and they learn differently. And yet men and women complement one another so beautifully that a healthy relationship makes both partners more complete. Consider the following ways that modern research has highlighted our uniqueness.

The differences start in the physical structure of the brain. "Now research is confirming that the brains of men and women are subtly different...For example, studies show that human male brains are, on average, approximately ten percent larger than female brains. Certain brain areas in women, however, contain more nerve cells."[5]

The differences then extend to the operation of the brain. "One study shows that men and women perform equally well in a test that asks subjects to read a list of nonsense words and determine if they rhyme. Yet, imaging results found that women use areas on the right and left sides of the brain, while men only use areas on the left side to complete the test."[6] We find it amusing that even when it comes to the use of the brain, women connect both sides while men keep it as simple as possible by using only one side.

It then follows that men and women excel at different tasks. "Tests show that women generally can recall lists of words or paragraphs of text better than men. On the other hand, men usually perform better on tests that require the ability to mentally rotate an image in order to solve a problem."[7] As a result, men use different strategies and different parts of their brains to navigate, and they really are better at finding their way when they are lost than women.

"Researchers scanned the brains of 12 men and 12 women as they tried to escape a three-dimensional virtual-reality maze. The volunteers pushed buttons to move their virtual selves left, right, or ahead. 'In the real world, that might be like trying to find a specific place in an unfamiliar city,' said neurologist Dr. Matthias Riepe of the University of Ulm in Germany. The men got out of the maze in an average of two minutes and 22 seconds, vs. an average of three minutes and 16 seconds for the women."[8] In regard to finding their way, men use geometry to figure it out, such as following a map, while women depend on their memory advantage and landmarks, such as "turn right at the drugstore." And it appears this difference is associated with the different parts of the brains that are used.[9]

Another interesting development in our understanding of male and female brains is that, "on average, that women synthesize the chemical serotonin at a lower level than men. Currently serotonin is a popular drug target because it has been implicated in a number of diseases, including depression."[10]

We find these differences fascinating. It is sometimes difficult having to adjust to your partner's ways, but it is also humorous and enjoyable. We have included below a list of ways that men and women approach life differently. Read through the list and see how many of them apply to your relationship:

- Men are more aggressive than women when they drive sports cars and light trucks. Women are more aggressive than men when they drive SUVs and luxury cars.[11]

• Most people believe men are safer drivers than women.[12]

• Women are less likely to be caught and convicted of speeding than men.[13]

• A research project was done on the quiz show *Jeopardy*. It was discovered that "men were more likely than women to appear as contestants, made most of the selections in the game, and won more money... Wagering strategies differed late in the game, as men bet a higher percent of their earnings than did women, but only when wagering on masculine topics."[14]

• When men perform as well as they expected at a particular task, they tend to attribute their success to their own skill or intelligence. If they perform below their expectations, they tend to blame it on bad luck or some factor that is out of their control.[15]

• When women meet their low expectations, they tend to attribute it to their lack of ability or intelligence. When women exceed their low prediction for achievement, they tend to attribute it to good luck or some other factor beyond their control.[16]

• Men, on average, are willing to take greater financial risks than women. "For example, in the 1989 Survey of Consumer Finances sponsored by the Federal Reserve System...Roughly 60% of the female respondents said they were not willing to accept any risk, while only 40% of the men said they were unwilling to take risks."[17]

• Women make safer choices than men when it comes to smoking, seat belt use, preventative dental care, and having regular blood pressure checks.[18]

• American men overwhelmingly feel that it's harder to be a guy today than it was 20 years ago and men are split on their opinion as to whether it's harder to be a woman than it was 20 years ago.[19]

• Within relationships, women resolve the day-to-day issues while men settle the life-changing disputes.[20]

• Women ask more questions.[21]

• More than three-fourths of interruptions in conversations are made by men.[22]

As you read this book, you will be exposed to the most important differences between you and your spouse. You will come across funny stories and jokes. We hope you will laugh with us, because developing a good sense of humor is one of the best ways to break the tension that exists in the battle of the sexes. Mostly, we hope you will gain insight into your mate and develop skills that will make you glad that men are like waffles and women are like spaghetti.

Here is a little quiz to help you see how well you understand the uniqueness each of you brings to your relationship:

Fun Questions for Married Couples

1. The recreational activity you most often do together is:
   A. Bicycling.
   B. Bowling.
   C. Hunting for his car keys.

2. Choose a vacation spot! Which qualifications for a prime vacation spot would appeal to the husband, and which would appeal to the wife?

    1. Quaint little shops.
    2. Golf, golf, golf.
    3. Nice restaurants.
    4. Big servings.
    5. Valet parking.
    6. Free parking.
    7. Room with a view.
    8. Room with a television set.
    9. Elegant sunken tub.
    10. Reading matter in the bathroom.

3. TRUE OR FALSE: A vacuum cleaner makes an excellent anniversary gift.

    TRUE! Provided you want it to be your last anniversary.

4. STORY PROBLEM: John and Betty must leave their home by 6 P.M. in order to be on time for a dinner party. John starts to get ready at 5:55 P.M. so he can leave at 6 P.M. What time does Betty need to start getting ready in order to leave by 6 P.M.?

    ANSWER: It makes no difference when Betty starts to get ready. She could start at 5 P.M., 4 P.M., or even 3 P.M. It doesn't matter. She's still going to be at least 20 minutes late.

5. (Husband question) When your wife says, "Let's not get each other Christmas presents this year," it indicates:

    A. Her desire to share with the less fortunate.
    B. Her thoughtful and realistic interest in the household budget.

C. A test to see if you "love her enough" to forget the suggestion and "surprise" her with something you'll be paying off until Columbus Day.

6. When a husband dons his almost-like-new coveralls and announces, "I'm going to work on the car," you can almost bet that:

A. Soon, it will purr like a kitten.
B. Soon, it will stop on a dime.
C. Soon, it will be towed to a nearby garage.

7. (Husband question) FILL IN THE BLANK: You can't make an omelet without:

A. Breaking some eggs.
B. Reading a recipe.
C. Hearing a lecture from your wife on the dangers of cholesterol.

8. Who is more likely to utter the following:

1. "What's for supper?"	Him	Her
2. "Have you seen my socks?"	Him	Her
3. "When are we leaving for church?"	Him	Her
4. "Do you think I've gained weight?"	Him	Her
5. "Where's the television schedule?"	Him	Her

9. Before answering the question "How do you like my new hairstyle?" what should a husband always remember?

A. His wife's feelings are the most important thing.
B. She may have spent hours in a salon to get it to look that way.
C. The couch is lumpy, and when you sleep on it a spring pokes you in the back.

10. His idea of the perfect honeymoon is:

A. A week in the Poconos.

B. A Mediterranean cruise.

C. Anything under a hundred bucks.

11. The phrase "not in your lifetime" refers to:

A. Him cleaning the bathroom.

B. Her cleaning out the gutters.

C. Either of you ever cleaning the stuff that grows under the vegetable crisper in the refrigerator.

12. When you think about the love letters you used to write when you were courting, you're reminded:

A. Of a passion that burned like ancient Rome.

B. Of a love that will last for eternity.

C. That writing corny love letters is not a crime.

13. Often men and women will show subtle signs of stress and strain in different ways. For each way listed below, choose the most appropriate gender.

1. Punch inanimate object, such as door or steering wheel.
   Male   Female   Either

2. Make sniffling noises and sigh heavily.
   Male   Female   Either

3. Blame clubs, bats, bowling balls, etc. for poor athletic performance.
   Male   Female   Either

4. Clamp hands over face and weep. When questioned, keep saying, "Oh, nothing" over and over.
   Male   Female   Either

14. When the both of you attend church together, it is best for the husband to wear:

A. A dark suit.

B. A tuxedo.

C. Whatever his wife picks out.

15. When the waiter asks what you'd like for dessert, a wife's most common response is:

    A. "Chocolate mousse, please."
    B. "I'll try the cheesecake."
    C. "Oh, nothing for me. I'll just have a teensie bite of his."

16. Your husband tries on his high school jacket and finds he can no longer snap it up. A wife's best response is:

    A. "Maybe it shrunk."
    B. "I like you a little less skinny."
    C. "That jacket would look dumb on a bald guy anyway."

17. Some household chores are traditionally done by the man, some by the woman. Place the following chores in the correct category:

	His	Hers
1. Cooking.	His	Hers
2. Flattening couch cushions.	His	Hers
3. Cleaning.	His	Hers
4. Tossing newspaper sections around.	His	Hers
5. Dusting.	His	Hers
6. Snoring on Saturday afternoon.	His	Hers

18. Your spouse is snoring. You should:

    A. Accept it as a minor flaw in an otherwise perfect mate.
    B. Gently nudge him and say, "Roll over, dear."
    C. Put a pair of sweatpants over his head and tighten the drawstring.

19. Who wants which addition to the house?

    1. A cozy breakfast nook.
       Wife   Husband
    2. A red velour wallpapered den with big leather couches and a pinball machine and a pool table and a moosehead

and a telephone that looks like a football helmet and a huge screen television set and a stereo with tapes of every college basketball game ever played and a train set and (well you get the idea)…

Wife   Husband

20. When riding with your husband on long car trips, you use the hours of quiet time to:

A. Discuss meaningful topics.

B. Point out the beauty of the scenery.

C. Excitedly warn him of impending highway danger that you can barely see as a tiny speck on the horizon.

21. If a longtime married couple is in the bathtub together, it can only mean:

A. They still feel passionately about each other.

B. Their love life is spontaneous and exciting.

C. He's grouting some loose tile while she tries to get rid of stubborn soap scum.

22. TRUE OR FALSE: The husband often lets his wife answer the telephone because it's usually for her anyway.

FALSE: The husband often lets his wife answer the telephone because, if he doesn't, he may end up talking to her mother.

23. The phrase most often heard when the two of you are alone in a quiet setting is:

A. "I love you."

B. "I need you."

C. "Zzzzzzzz…"

24. When doing the laundry, which of the following is the average husband most likely to forget?

A. Whites in hot.

B. Colors in cold.

C. Pens, pencils, keys, tissues, etc. in pockets.

25. A husband offers to run to the store for a quart of milk. He is most likely to return with:

A. A quart of milk.

B. Two steaks, a big fish, a bottle of ketchup, two bottles of pop, a box of donuts, a TV dinner, some cheese, the latest issue of *TV Guide*, and a can of 40-weight motor oil.

C. A dazed expression and the question, "What was I supposed to get?"

26. (Husband question) To prove your love for your wife, you would gladly:

A. Climb the highest mountain.

B. Swim the deepest ocean.

C. Hold her purse while she tries things on at the mall and run the risk that, at any moment, one of the guys might walk by.

27. (Wife question) To prove your love for your husband, you would gladly:

A. Climb the highest mountain.

B. Swim the deepest ocean.

C. Put gas in the car at one of those self-serve places where the risk of a broken fingernail is a constant threat.[23]

2

Waffles and Spaghetti Communicating

Don't Overcook Communication

"If I say something that can be interpreted in two ways, and one of the ways makes you sad or angry, I meant the other way."

A couple came to a counselor because they were on the brink of divorce. The counselor asked the wife, "Does your husband beat you up?"

She answered, "No, I beat him up by several hours every morning."

Then the counselor asked the husband, "Do you have a grudge?"

The husband responded, "No, we have a carport."

The counselor, getting a little exasperated, asked the couple, "What grounds do you have for your problems?"

The wife answered, "We have about four acres."

Finally the counselor said, "Why did you come in here today?"

Together they said, "We can't seem to communicate."

Houston, We Have a Problem

Men and women have very different approaches to communication. When a man starts a conversation, it is generally because he perceives there is a problem that needs to be addressed. If there is no perceived problem, he feels no particular need to talk. The box he is currently in is at ease, and the lack of distress makes him assume that everything is all right with the relationship. His wife, on the other hand, has a constant desire to talk with her husband. She wants to connect him to everything in her life and assumes he wants to connect her to everything in his life. When she begins a conversation, he assumes she is bringing up a problem that needs to be resolved. Generally, she is starting the conversation because it seems natural to talk about whatever is on her mind. While she is in conversational mode, he turns on the "fix-it" mechanism and the conflict begins. She gets her feelings hurt because he is trying to figure her out rather than just visit with her. He gets impatient because there seems to be no point. What started out as a hopeful moment for drawing closer together becomes another nagging defeat.

So how does a couple make communication work for them? We believe the most important communication skill a couple can develop is to learn to take turns.

Follow the Leader

Whoever begins a specific conversation should be the one to set the pace for the conversation. Let me (Bill) talk with the men first. When your wife begins a conversation with you, assume that she needs to connect the issues of her life together. She doesn't need you to work your male logic into her thinking process. She simply needs you to help her make the connections. You will do well if you view the conversation as a journey she is going to lead you on. Pack your bags, go on the journey, and encourage her to take the conversation wherever she wants. Many men refuse to do this because they are afraid that if they give their wives permission to talk until they are done, the end will never come. This just isn't true. Most men don't know this, however, because they have never helped their wives finish a conversation.

Your wife is driven to connect. Because she is aware of all the issues of her life, and because it is impossible to fix every issue in her life all at once, she approaches things differently than you. Before she looks for solutions, she interacts with each part of her life and experiences the appropriate emotion of each issue. Things she should be upset with, she gets upset about. Things that are sentimental bring soft words and flowing tears. Things that are exciting bring giggles and enthusiasm. Things that are intense bring focused concentration. Each issue gets its own emotional reaction. That is why she can experience such a range of emotions in one conversation. Just because you, as a man, cannot keep up with her does not mean that your way is better. If you are willing to serve this need of hers, you will be married to a much happier woman. You will know when she is done connecting things together because she will let out a deep sigh and may say something like, "You understand me like no one else in the world," or "You are my best friend. Thanks." You may not really understand what she is going through, but it will definitely make her life better.

A common complaint for men is that their wives ramble on… and on…and on…and on, seemingly with no point. Because they cannot figure out where the conversation is going, they feel powerless to do anything about it. A sense of failure sets in, and he concludes his wife is unreasonable and unable to think through issues.

Going the Distance

A new perspective is needed. Men, to help you understand your wife's need to finish conversations, imagine if everything in your life ended early. What if you were never able to finish a meal because it was taken away from you when you were halfway through? What if every sporting event you watched on TV was turned off five minutes before the end of the game? What if every sexual encounter ended before its climax? What if every project you started had to be abandoned before you were able to finish it? How are you feeling? Can you sense the frustration and irritation this would bring? If life were actually like this, your anger would always be close to the surface, and your motivation to keep pursuing these activities would be shattered.

This is the way your wife feels when she is not able to finish conversations with you. She experiences the same frustration and irritation. Her motivation to keep talking is threatened but her need to talk with you won't go away. She builds up hope that this time you will be interested, only to have it shattered by your insistence on getting to the point. The game has ended early, and the project must be left unfinished and unattended. You can avoid this irritating chain of events by simply taking some time to listen to your wife on a regular basis. She will keep things more connected, and your life will be easier.

I shared this concept at a conference with a number of couples, and one of the men left more than a little frustrated. He accepted his wife's need to connect everything in her life, but he couldn't figure out a practical plan for helping her. As he continued to ponder the issue, it occurred to him that he could develop a listening box. In this box, he defined the problem and invented a solution. The problem was his wife needed to actively visit with him, and the solution was for him to listen to her for half an hour at a time. He now sets the goal of listening to his wife for 30 minutes at a sitting. If he succeeds, he rejoices because he conquered the challenge, and she rejoices because she has connected more of her life to him.

Stay in the Box

Ladies, when it is your husband's turn to talk, you need to practice staying in the box he wants to open. You see, when he brings up an issue for discussion, he actually intends to talk about that issue. So when he says to you, "We need to talk about our finances," he most likely wants to have a financial conversation. If he says he wants to talk about your upcoming vacation, he probably wants to talk about your vacation, and so on. He is hoping this time will be different. He wants to have what he considers to be a reasonable conversation with you. He wants it to stay on track. He wants to identify the problem, evaluate the options, commit to a solution, and see it work out.

A problem develops because you immediately recognize all the issues that are related to the one he brought up. It is as if you can see every box that is touching the box he has opened. You feel the need to open all those boxes because they are relevant to the discussion. If you don't open them, you are afraid the loose ends will never be addressed. You know that it has backfired in the past, but you haven't ever really understood why, so you try again.

The problem is we women are very impatient listeners. We often think that because men don't process life the way we do they are unfeeling and uncaring, but nothing could be further from the truth. The fact is, we never let them stay in one box long enough to discover their feelings. One cartoon I saw explains how we usually view men and their feelings.

A niece came into the room where her uncle was sitting in his recliner. He had done some favors for her, and she wanted to express her thanks. The young woman rambled on and on, "Thank you so much, you always come through for me. What would I do without you…"

The uncle finally took a business card out of his pocket, gave it to his niece, and said, "If you take this down to the petroleum store they will give you ten percent off your petroleum."

His wife witnessed the interaction and later said, "What were you doing? She was pouring her heart out to you and you gave her a business card? Have you no feelings?"

"I have feelings. I was *afraid* she was going to hug me, I was *scared* it was going to go on and on, and I was *happy* when it was over! I have feelings!"

If we stay focused on one topic and resist the urge to open up all the surrounding boxes, we buy our men the emotional time they need to work their way down through the layers of the box. They then trust us enough to open up the well of emotions that are deep in that box. It's a lot like drilling for oil. When you drill deep enough, you can reach a valuable gusher! We ladies must remember that we are drilling for valuable treasure, not interrogating a prisoner. Patient listening will periodically bring the emotions to the surface we love to see.

I (Pam) was visiting with a young lady in our church who was engaged to be married. She asked if she could speak with me because she was concerned about her upcoming marriage. She loved her fiancé deeply, but she was afraid that he was kind of shallow. He loved cars and spent most of his free time in the garage working on the next automobile project he had lined up. He was kind to her and respected the things she said, but he seemed to be dominated by cars.

"Pam, I love him. What am I supposed to do? How can I know for sure?"

"Go into the garage," I enthusiastically told her. "It is obvious this is his favorite box. He feels confident there. Meet him there and see what happens."

Well, two weeks later I saw her again, and she was so excited. She had taken some lemonade into the garage where he was working on his car and just sat and listened to him. He was talking about torquing this and tweaking that. He was using vocabulary like "horsepower" and "compression," words that were meaningless to her. She described how her eyes were rolling back in her head from boredom when he suddenly dropped into a new box.

"Thank you so much for caring about me," he said as he gave her a quick kiss on the cheek. "No one has ever taken the time to listen to me like you. You are the only person I have ever known who has let me go on and on about my cars without getting bored. I can picture myself growing old with you. We are going to have a great life together."

With that he gave her a big hug and then went back to working on his car.

She was so touched by the connection she received after the ordeal of listening that she said to me, "Pam, I am never leaving the garage again."

The Emergency Shut-off Valve

When your husband started the conversation, there was one problem on the table to be solved. When you opened the second box, there were two problems. When you opened the third box, there were three, and so on. Every man has his own limit of how many problems he can deal with at once. Because he started the conversation, he is in the problem-solving mode, and so every box you open feels like a separate problem to him. At some point, he crosses the line of how many issues he can handle, and he gets overwhelmed.

A man's reactions to being overwhelmed can be varied, but they seem to fall into two categories. He either shuts down or gets angry. If your husband's tendency is to shut down, he may walk away from the conversation or give you the silent treatment. He feels there is no way he can succeed, so he loses motivation. He doesn't know how to keep up with you and thinks he is going to lose the conversation. The only way he can get on level playing ground with you is to bail out.

If your husband's tendency is to get angry, he might throw accusations at you, storm out of the house and disappear for a while, or aggressively call off the conversation by telling you to stop talking. The whole time he is telling himself he should not be this angry, but he feels lost and doesn't know how to recover his composure. Rather than expose his lack of control, he protects himself from any further feelings of inadequacy by becoming upset. The end result of either of these approaches is failed communication.

Don't Make Me You

Instead of taking turns listening to each other, most couples spend their time trying to change one another. As his wife is breaking down the walls that allow him to separate the issues in his life, he is trying to cut up her spaghetti into squares. They are sincerely trying to make sense of each other, but they only end up confusing each other more. It is as if she is putting marinara sauce on the waffles, and he is putting syrup on the spaghetti of their lives.

Taking turns may be hard work, but not taking turns is agonizing. For the couple who wants to find a way to make their differences work *for* them in communication, they must become good listeners. The amazing thing is that the same listening techniques work for both sides. For the man who wants to be able to travel in conversation with his wife, he must be a focused listener. For the wife who wants to be able to camp in the same box her husband is in, she must be a focused listener.

First, let's take a look at what listening is not.

Listening is not an attempt to understand the opposite sex. We have been told numerous times that true intimacy is attained when a couple understands one another. The problem is that a man will never fully understand a woman and a woman will never fully understand a man. I (Bill) cannot understand what it is like to be a woman because I am not a woman. I will never understand what it is like to be raised by an alcoholic father. I will never know the tension of putting my career on hold for eight years while I was waiting for my kids to start school. The only way I can relate to these influences in my wife's life is to listen to her and let her explain to me what it is like to be Pam. Many partners are disappointed with each other because they believed that love meant understanding and they failed to achieve it. When the closeness they were promised is missing, they conclude they weren't meant for each other or that they just don't have what it takes.

Listening is not an attempt to become each other's counselor. Good listening does not always start with you leaning toward your spouse, looking deeply into his or her eyes and, with a compassionately whiney voice, asking, "How are you feeling today?" There is a time and place for counseling, but it usually is not in the midst of your everyday responsibilities. When something is wrong in your circumstances or some transition of life is getting the better of you, it is wise to schedule time with a counselor who can provide a strategic environment for analyzing your growth.

Listening is not an attempt to fix your partner. Avoid asking, "Why do you feel this way?" The answer is often, "I don't know." Our emotions have never had the ability to think. We feel what we feel because of past influences and developmental progress. Emotions are not rational in their makeup—they don't think before they express themselves. The goal in intimate conversation with your spouse is not to analyze emotions and come up with some kind of solution that will make him or her never feel this way again. The goal is to grow a little closer and reaffirm your love. This love you share with your spouse can be worn down over time. If you are not careful to reaffirm it often, it loses its vitality and can be swallowed up in life. When, on the other hand, you maintain the habit of often reestablishing the bond of love that drew you together, you will experience a growing joy with each other.

Your husband may say, "I am often intimidated by my boss." Try not to respond with, "There is no reason to be intimidated. You are bright, intelligent, and talented. Your boss is just threatened by how good you are. Be brave, honey. It will be all right!" In doing so, you shut him down. Your husband is probably trying to get a conversation started with you that is bigger than work. It probably has to do with his lack of confidence or lack of understanding of how competition works in an adult world. Or he may be contemplating a job change, and he is checking to see how accepting you may be of having that conversation. Or he may be intimidated by you, and he is trying to lead into the conversation by blaming his boss first! Whatever the case may be, you will never know if you attempt to fix him rather than let him work the process with your listening help.

Listening is not a personality trait. You do not have to become someone else in order to listen to your spouse. Listening is a skill, just like driving or typing or music. You must practice and, over time, develop your own style. The basic elements of listening—attentiveness, empathy, and compassionate questions —are shared by all good listeners, but no two people listen exactly the same. Two guitar players will sound a little different even though they are playing the same song, and two drivers will have different styles of driving even though they arrive at the same destination. Your ability to listen strategically is determined by how much value you place on it and how hard you are willing to work at it. And in the end, you, will develop your own style of listening that will fit well in your lifestyle and will captivate your spouse's heart.

Levels of Communication

Now let's define what listening *is*. To understand the kind of listening that builds healthy marriages, we must first understand that communication takes place on four levels.

The first level is small talk. This is where you deal with the straightforward stuff of life. "How is the weather?" "What do we need from the store?" "Who is picking up the kids and taking them to practice?" It is important that small talk remain relatively uncomplicated. If you begin asking questions, such as, "Honey, how do feel about going to the store to get milk?" or "Does it freak you out that it might rain today?" communication will wear you out. Issues like the weather and groceries need to be handled as simply and nonemotionally as possible.

The second is the level of thoughts and opinions. These areas require a little more than the obvious, but they are not inherently emotional. Questions like, "Where would you like to go to dinner tonight?" "What is your favorite color?" "Which outfit do you like better?" are questions that should not throw a couple into a tailspin. We should provide freedom to one another to have our own opinions on these issues without loading them up with emotional freight. This, however, seems to be the level at which most couples get in trouble. We test one another's commitment to the relationship at this point. We ponder thoughts like, *Doesn't he know what color I like best? Doesn't he care enough to remember where I like to eat? Why can't she just accept that I like to watch sports? I wish she would wear things I like.* When we allow this to develop, we expend so much emotional energy dealing with the simple aspects of life that we never get to enjoy further steps of intimacy.

The third level is where people share their opinions and convictions. This is where spiritual and moral convictions are revealed to one another. This is the level at which compatibility is vital for married couples. It is impossible to establish compatibility in all areas of life. Your gender differences, personality differences, family backgrounds, and personal preferences guarantee that some parts of your relationship will be incompatible, but you don't need to see eye to eye in every area. You do, however, need significant agreement on the core issues of life. If you differ on your preference for hobbies or your favorite colors or the level to which you like to have your house organized, you will most likely continue to get along and find workable compromises. If, however, you differ on the role of God in your life, your moral values, or your methods of parenting, your relationship will be defined by conflict.

The fourth level is the area of emotional intimacy. This is the level where you and your spouse give one another insight into who you are that no one else gets to see. It is where you share your dreams, your fantasies, your fears, the ridiculous ways you think and feel, and the things in your life you are most proud of. This is the area where couples must be deliberate if they are going to make headway, because every step in level four is vulnerable. Life will *require* you to communicate at the first three levels. You only reach level four if you *choose* to go there.

"You haven't heard a word I have been saying!" shouted Jeannie.

"What are you talking about?" returned Blake with obvious frustration in his voice. "We've been talking for over an hour, and you think I haven't been listening? I just think you are being too emotional!"

"How would you know if I am emotional? You haven't ever heard one single beat of my heart," Jeannie blurted out, knowing her words would inflame the conversation. "I thought you were special, but you really are just like any other man. How can I ever trust you if you won't listen to me?"

"Whoa! You are really hurt about this, aren't you?" responded Blake, desperately looking for some way to turn the conversation around. "I thought I was trying hard to talk to you more."

"You *have* been talking to me more. You just haven't been listening!"

Listen to Key Words and Phrases

Blake and Jeannie are stuck at a point where many couples find themselves. They are spending quite a bit of time talking to each other, but they seem to be getting nowhere in their relationship. They want to connect, but in all their talking they don't know how to listen in a way that creates intimacy. We can all face this situation when we become slow communicators. We throw out hints rather than boldly telling our spouses how we are doing. As we learn to respond to these "hints," we can encourage our spouse to reveal more of what is really going on in his or her heart.

When it comes to this type of disclosure, it has been our experience that people reveal themselves in stages. They start out with "safe" statements and progressively share more risky and vulnerable truths if the atmosphere of the conversation is conducive.

The key principle in promoting intimacy, then, is giving permission to your spouse to share at a vulnerable level. If your spouse senses permission to share without being judged or prematurely "fixed," new information will emerge. This new information will lead you to a better understanding of what your spouse is all about at the emotional level of life that motivates actions and decisions. The skills that grant permission to your spouse are:

1. Repeat the key words or phrases he or she says with the voice inflection that says, "I have heard what you said, and I am ready to listen to more."

2. After your spouse has been talking for a few minutes with your encouragement, summarize his or her thoughts and then ask, "Is that what you have been saying?"

3. After a significant amount of sharing, when you think you have a good idea of what is motivating your spouse, describe a time in your life when you think you have felt the same way. When you are done describing this event, ask your spouse, "Is that what it is like for you?"

"Let's try again," Blake said, reaching out and holding Jeannie's hands in a way that says, "You're safe with me." "You mentioned that I don't listen. Tell me what you mean by that."

"I tell you how I feel, and you just tell me how I should act," Jeannie cautiously said.

"So I just tell you how you should act?" Blake responded with a reassuring curiosity in his voice.

"Blake, when you tell me what to do as if it is a simple thing, you make me feel stupid." Jeannie was hesitatingly becoming more vulnerable.

"I make you feel stupid?" Blake asked with genuine surprise in his voice. He had always thought Jeannie was one of the brightest people he had ever met.

She sensed his genuine concern and was amazed at herself when she blurted out, "It makes me feel the same way my parents used to when they told me I was an accident and they wished I'd never been born."

"They told you that?" Blake's astonishment was obvious to Jeannie. They had been married for five years, and Blake was amazed that he had never heard about this before.

"I was 16. I couldn't believe it at first when my dad said it. We were having this really big fight. I was being pretty difficult, I admit, but I don't think I deserved that. I looked at my mom and asked if it was true that I was an accident—that I was unwanted. When she just looked down at the ground in silence, I felt my heart fall through my feet. I've tried hard to cover up my pain all these years, but it keeps coming back to haunt me. Whenever you treat me as though I don't know what I am doing, I feel that same pain again."

"I am sorry, Jeannie. I didn't know."

"I know, Blake. I try to tell myself that you don't mean to make me feel this way, but sometimes it just overwhelms me. I didn't know whether to tell you or just be angry with you to protect myself."

As Blake embraced Jeannie, he marveled at the new sense of warmth and trust in their relationship. He convinced himself that night he would be wise if he learned how to listen more.

100 to 1 Principle

Sometimes it isn't easy to discover ways to encourage a spouse. One woman came to me and said, "There is nothing here! No spark, or sizzle—nothing! I have no feelings. I want out of this marriage!"

I suggested that we pray and ask God to show her one positive thing about her spouse. She went home and prayed some more. The next day she called me and said, "I thought of something."

"Good, what is it?" I asked hopefully.

"He's still here."

He's still here! I thought she was kidding, but I could tell from her tone that she was completely serious.

"Okay, let's run with that. Let's brainstorm together ways you can tell him thanks for being here—but in a positive manner."

We made a list of several ways to positively say, "You're here!" and she went back home and began to use them. She would see her husband sitting in his recliner with the remote in hand watching sports. She'd walk by and rub his shoulders and say, "It's nice to know you're around."

She'd see him sitting reading the paper, and walk by and say, "You know, I was thinking, it's nice to know some things in life you can count on—like you being here."

She came up with so many ways to positively say, "You're here, bud," that one day he got up out of that old recliner! He came into the living room where she was having a quiet time, reading her Bible. He had never been interested in spiritual discussions before this, but he said, "Honey, what are you reading?"

"My Bible. I was having a problem at work and this passage in the Psalms is helping me."

"Why don't you read it to me?" She did and added an explanation of how it applied to her life.

"That's pretty neat," he replied with genuine enthusiasm in his voice.

The next Sunday, a miracle happened. Instead of going to his favorite chair, he asked if he could go to church with her—and he has been going ever since. In addition, she now regularly tells me of his romantic gestures toward her.

She found the power of encouraging words by taking 100 percent of her energy and focusing it on one positive trait. Our experience has taught me that happiness and passion in marriage do not come from *finding* the right partner, but in *being* the right partner.

> I once heard about a woman who was unhappy in her marriage and angry at her husband. When she went to her lawyer to begin divorce proceedings, she asked his advice on what she could do to really hurt her lousy husband. The lawyer thought for a moment and suggested that for the next couple of months, she love him and romance him with every ounce of her being and once he was happy and fulfilled, she serve him with the divorce papers. "It will rip his heart out," the lawyer promised.

> The woman followed his advice. Several months later, she returned to the lawyer's office. He handed her the divorce papers to examine before serving them to her husband, and the woman replied, "I won't be needing them now. We're getting ready to leave on our second honeymoon."[1]

The power of encouraging words, try some of your own today.

3

Waffles and Spaghetti Relaxing

Remote Places and Remote Controls

" Let your boat of life be light, packed with only what you need—a homely home and simple pleasures, one or two friends worthy of the name, someone to love and someone to love you... "

—Jerome K. Jerome

When I (Pam) was a little girl, I used to spend the summer on my grandparents' farm. My grandparents had a deep love for one other, but sometimes, as with any couple, life's circumstances didn't go quite as anticipated. In those stressful moments, I witnessed coping patterns in my grandparents that worked quite well for them during their 60 plus years together. Now, as an adult relationship educator, I realize their pattern was quite common! But it was their acceptance of this pattern that was uncommon—and it produced a long-lasting marital relationship.

The scenario from a child's point of view seemed quite simple: A crisis would happen and almost instantaneously Grandma would begin to cook something—or at the very least clean something in the kitchen. She held back her tears, and sometimes her rage and anger, by cooking and cleaning up a storm. If my mother or any other woman was around, Grandma would start talking her way through the situation—and if no one was in sight, she would pick up the phone to chat. While she was working and talking, Grandpa quietly made his way to his shop.

As a child, I never could understand why Grandpa wanted to spend so much time in that "dirty ol' shop." It reeked of oil and dust. Everywhere you looked was a tool or a gadget. Little did I realize then that this was a sanctuary for my grandfather's soul. While Grandma would cook and talk, do dishes and talk, iron and talk to debrief and handle stress, Grandpa tinkered and created in his shop. Every kind of tool known to mankind was in that shop. In fact, Grandpa had to triple its size because his garage just wouldn't do! Walls of wrenches, pliers, saws, and ratchets hung in carefully patterned rows. There were drawers and drawers of tiny parts and just as many drawers of power tools. Martha Stewart might say his shop was decorated in Craftsman Red. He could stay out there all day because he had a little refrigerator and freezer packed with Grandma's prize-winning cookies. He had some old tractor seats he'd used to create a male conversation area, warmed with a potbellied stove right in the center. That way, men without shops could run to this place of retreat when they were in the doghouse with their wives.

If Grandpa stormed out to the shop angry, it magically calmed his frustrations and fears. As he'd work, he'd think. As he tinkered, he would review, problem solve, and reflect on not only the problem, but the people involved. We grandkids knew enough not to follow him right out to the shop. We would wait about 30 minutes, then we would be invited into his holy place.

We'd prop ourselves on the car hood, or on one of those tractor seats or the workbench, and listen to Grandpa's stories. Telling stories always made him smile and say nice things about Grandma, no matter how upset he had been in the kitchen. In the shop he'd find his emotional center. He would never confess that was what he was doing! He'd say he was workin', but we all knew better! When Grandpa finally made his way back inside for supper, the problem-solving conversations my grandparents would have were in hushed, calm, and rational voices. Once they reached this point, their differences were rather quickly solved.

Do You Have a Minute?

When stress hits, women need to traverse across all those noodles and emotionally connect to the people and situations connected to the problem at hand. Because women are more "in tune" with the emotional and relational nuances of life, they report more anxiety overall.[1] It is generally well known in the clinical domain that post-adolescent females suffer a higher incidence of depression than their male counterparts. They also experience a higher incidence of anxiety disorders. In fact, "females have higher levels of neurochemicals linked to panic and anticipatory anxiety than their male counterparts."[2] Moreover, women produce lower levels of serotonin in their bodies, which raises their genetic vulnerability to depression. As a result, women are prone to higher levels of depression-related anxiety than are men.[3] In short, women have more to deal with when it comes to managing stress. Not only do they seek solutions for the situations that need improving, they also have a flood of emotions to process.

For this reason, talking is a huge help to a woman. As she talks through the stress of her life, the emotions associated with the circumstances dissipate. The climate of her life gets clearer as she expresses the emotional weather of her heart. Solutions begin to emerge and simpler approaches appear as possibilities. It is as if stress catapults her into an emotional fog bank. Before she can navigate the course, she needs to clear the fog by talking her way through. Her conversational roadmap can include God, friends, extended family, and her husband. The combination of people she talks with may change with each situation, but the key is she must talk her way out of stress.

In an attempt to guarantee the opportunity to talk, women will often act out to get the attention of her husband. Mom will often get busy in the kitchen. You'll hear pots and pans clanging, or she'll decide to spring clean the house from top to bottom. I call this the Mighty Martyr Syndrome. You've thought it before: *I'm the only one who can do anything around here. I am upset and angry and hurt, so I think I will just slam all these cupboards open and shut very loudly and maybe that will wake up my emotionally dead-headed husband and he will come in and ask me what is wrong!*

I've been so upset at night that I make myself cry out loud, hoping my sobs will wake Bill. And if that doesn't work, I have been known to toss the covers back so hard that the blankets make enough noise to wake him up! Because I need to de-stress through conversation, I will go to great lengths to try to get Bill's attention! However, none of the games I play work very well. So for the most part, I have opted to use a saner method. "Honey, I need to talk for a few minutes. Something is upsetting me. Can you take some time and come sit with me?" He's much more motivated to sit and listen to me when I come to him in honesty and calmness, rather than as a woman who could be mistaken for an actress auditioning for a melodrama!

Bingo and Other Boxes

Men, on the other hand, in times of stress retreat to easy boxes. Every man has certain boxes in his life that are much easier on him emotionally than others. When he enters these boxes, life melts away and he has an opportunity to recharge. Men do not get energized by constantly processing life. In fact, it drains them of energy. They get ready for the next challenge by disappearing into a stress-free box for a period of time. They emerge from that box energized, focused, and able to conquer the next obstacle.

What are some of the easy boxes? Many men find that sports (either playing or watching) is a very effective stress reliever. They can get lost in the game for a time and ignore the overwhelming responsibilities of life. Other men find a computer, or other recreational technologies, a male-friendly way to reduce the anxiety of life. Others disappear into a good book or music. Still others immerse themselves in projects that require their undivided attention.

How do we recognize a man's easy boxes? It seems that God helped us ladies out a bit with this one. Men's easy boxes are generally shaped like boxes. A newspaper is shaped like a box. A TV screen is shaped like a box. A basketball court and a football field are shaped like boxes. A computer screen is shaped like a box. And the favorite of all men's safe, easy boxes—a bed—is, of course, shaped like a box!

So sleep and sex are two preferred coping mechanisms of the male gender, and of these two, sex is often a man's favorite easy box. If a man's life were pictured as a bingo card with all those rows of boxes, the sex box would be the free space in the center of the card. It is larger than all the other boxes, and a man can get there from pretty much every other box on the card!

It is not difficult to see that this could cause trouble for the couple who does not have a deliberate plan to relieve stress. The wife feels the need to talk things out while her husband would prefer to play. She wants conversation while he wants a safe retreat or, better yet, to have sex before taking a nap!

Take Turns Coping

When stress hits our relationship, especially stress from outside circumstances, Bill and I have a habit of asking each other, "How are you doing?" I might ask, "Bill, do you need to play some one-on-one basketball before you'll have the energy to listen to my heart?" Or if I know life is particularly stressful on him, and I feel emotionally up to it, I will whisper in his ear, "Come on, I have something for you." Then I'll lead him to the bedroom expecting nothing for myself, only wanting to give him a gift of satisfying sex.

Or, if he is handling the stress better than I am, he'll whisk me away, even for a few hours, so we can exercise or walk and talk or have a meal together. All he does is listen and hold me, tenderly caressing my cares away. And if he listens really well, BINGO!

Coping Skills

Go to God first. When stress feels like it is piling up inside you, go to God first and unleash your fears and frustrations. Fear is often a component of the stress we experience. When we have no good way to calm fear we further complicate the situation. Women typically express their feelings with more confrontational and hostile styles. Because women can become emotional under stress, it is easy for women to say and do things that exacerbate the problem rather than make it better. Words just roll out—hurtful words, heated words—and the damage that can be done by them should not be underestimated. Men, on the other hand, tend to turn their fear inward and put more stress on their bodies. As a result, fear has been shown to contribute to more health problems in men than women.[4]

God's shoulders are big enough to handle your deepest and darkest fears and frustrations. You don't have to worry about saying things you might never be able to get back or saying things that might "wound" God. He can't be wounded. He knows all you are feeling and thinking anyway. By going to God first, you gain an emotional release and the clarity to think and talk things through. This dress rehearsal with him better prepares you to succeed on the stage of life.

Deliberately help your wife talk things out. The following approaches can help your wife talk through the anxiety of her current circumstances and bring her back to the woman you married.

1. Offer to listen. Say, "It seems like you are pretty upset. Tell me what's going on in your mind."

2. Touch her. Gently pick up her hand, stroke her arm, wrap your arms around her. Start with a small amount of touch and if it calms her, give more. Bill will say to me, "Honey, it'll be okay," and he'll just hold me as I sob into his strong chest with his arms wrapped around me.

3. Offer help. "Honey, what can I do to help?" "You want to take a minute and brainstorm to see what would help?" "Let's pitch in and help mom." These are all welcome phrases to a stressed-out woman.

4. Own up to it. If *you* are the problem because you broke a promise or dropped the ball on a responsibility, saying I'm sorry does help—especially when accompanied by the top three—and flowers! (And maybe a gift certificate!)

Deliberately encourage your husband to spend time in easy boxes. Your husband needs some time to get involved in mindless activity when stress hits your home. If you give him permission to go and are generally glad that he has the opportunity, he will go without guilt and will be drawn toward you in the midst of the stress.

In our home, when life becomes very, very stressful and we are tempted to blame one another, instead we say, "It's not you, it's not me—it's just life." By taking each other off the hook, we can be a unified team and tackle the problems together.

Take a step back. Come apart before you come apart. One of the best ways to cope with stress is to get away from it. Taking a step back can help you gain rest, perspective, and a second wind. Any stress is easier to go through when you are emotionally connected as a couple. Getting away does two things: it shrinks a woman's world (less noodles to deal with), and it is a favorite coping strategy of men—retreat, relax, and reconnect sexually. Depending on the stress and circumstances, different kinds of getaways are in order.

The Great Getaway

Sometimes, getting away from it all is the best way to romance your mate. Guys, shrink her world down or plan a weekend away where she is free to talk and talk and talk. By listening, you'll sweep her off her feet. Let her shop a little and pick up a few things for the kids and you'll be a hit.

Ladies, plan a weekend away where you never leave the hotel room, never get dressed—never leave the bed—and you'll be a hit! Or at least keep the expectations low: golf, dinner, sex; parasail, dinner, sex; Jet ski, dinner, sex—getting the drift?

The R and R Getaway

Time off for rest and relaxation. Time to do absolutely nothing. Lie in the sun, read novels, recreate, and slow down. Couples who live a fully packed, fast-paced life are wise to build these breaks into their schedules on a regular basis. Those in the helping professions (social workers, counselors, doctors and nurses, pastors) are happier and healthier when they carve out quiet, nonpeople getaways. Bill and I aim at having a 24-hour oasis quarterly. One man, nearing retirement in a people-helping profession, told his protégé, "Steal your wife away to a hotel for 24 hours once a month, and you'll always have a great marriage and a good sex life." Sometimes scheduling every aspect of life is what has you down, so be spontaneous. Pack a toothbrush, some lingerie, and a bathing suit and head out! Let your whims carry you.

- Try flipping a coin to decide left or right or north or south.

- Choose a city, but go to the tourist bureau or Chamber of Commerce to see what the most unique, most economical accommodations might be.

- Pretend to kidnap your sweetheart. Call ahead and book appointments under a false name with his or her secretary, then walk in with a blindfold and steal your love away to some surprise getaway location. You have to plan, but your spouse, who may be under extreme pressure, will appreciate the "unplan."

- Leave your watches at home. Sleep when you're tired and eat when you're hungry.

- Go on an off day. Often Tuesday through Thursday is less expensive in tourist towns, and weekends can be less expensive at hotels that cater to business clientele.

A Planning Getaway

Once a year, Bill and I set aside time away to talk over the business side of our life. We set goals, talk finances, plan for the children's needs, and do calendaring and scheduling for the year. This alleviates many arguments because we are both operating off the same agenda. This time away is when we discuss expectations we have on each other. We talk over career plans, business items, pace of life—anything that either of us sees as a challenge to be overcome. By taking these regular planning getaways, we keep our anniversary and birthday getaways free from distractions—and we can really enjoy each other rather than have the mood ruined by a business item.

In *Pure Pleasure: Making Your Marriage a Great Affair* (Intervarsity Press), we give some suggestions for maintaining "Love Under Pressure." To get the most relaxation and direction out of your planning getaway try these helpful principles:

Set a date, then delegate. Share the responsibility for making reservations, child care arrangements, and any other details. Decide who will do what. You don't want to start fighting before you ever leave town!

Play and pray. Plan a fun activity, a nap, or a good meal before you begin setting goals or making decisions. Try praying as a couple and ask God to help you plan. You'll be less likely to battle for territory or argue over small priorities after you've asked God to be a part.

Put first things first. Remind yourself of your life priorities. If you've never written a mission statement for your marriage, start there. What values and priorities are important to you two? What would you like written on your tombstone after you're gone? It's worth the time. Having a plan for your marriage will build trust and confidence!

The Surprise Getaway

This is a sure way to keep the spontaneity in a relationship. We "plan" our surprises! That is, on each other's birthdays we seek to do something out of the ordinary. Take turns planning your getaways so that one of you is always surprised. These take a lot of preparation on the part of the one doing the "whisking" and a lot of flexibility on the part of the one being "whisked."

The Un-Getaway

This is the most creative and easiest getaway to regularly make a part of your lifestyle. These are the quick overnighters when the kids go to Grandma's or a friend's, and you make your place an instant hotel. This idea takes away the excuse, "We can't afford it." Even a night curled up together on the sofa, watching a romantic movie followed by a morning of sleeping in, can be a welcome relief for busy couples.

Make it different. Turn your room into a cozy bed-and-breakfast by stringing a set of small twinkling Christmas lights around your ceiling—you'll create a starlight atmosphere with more privacy. Buy all the foods you never eat. Maybe a theme would be more romantic. Borrow plants and turn your patio into a Hawaiian paradise. Splurge for two breakfast trays and some satin sheets and spend the getaway in your room.

Make it private. Unplug technology. Turn off the phones, pagers, PC's. Park cars in the garage or down the block so you don't look like you're home. Put a note on your front door instructing people to come back after a certain time. One couple even hung a "Quarantined" sign in the window!

Make it personal. Write a poem, pull out photo albums, buy a new music tape, or plan a quiet movie or game that is your spouse's favorite! Each of you come up with a personal touch beforehand. Rent her favorite video. Wear his favorite nightie.

The Building Getaway

This is for marriage tune-ups and enrichment. If you build into your love life before the crisis hits, you'll find that no crisis can tear you two apart! Some couples choose to visit a marriage counselor once a year for a marriage checkup, then they go on to a self-run enrichment weekend where they read a book together, do a Bible study, or watch or listen to marriage videos or audio tapes. The key to a healthy marriage-building getaway is to choose positive input. Choose one that values commitment, a couple's uniqueness, and includes information and exercises to build a couple's spiritual, emotional, and physical life.

Each conference is like a good investment in your future. Just like an IRA or Keogh helps you at retirement, so a structured or semi-structured conference will pay big dividends when the pressure is on later in "real" life. To get the most out of a weekend conference:

Come early. Relax together the night before or early in the afternoon around the pool.

Do the activities and communication exercises. Try to focus on your spouse rather than the other people around you.

Stay late. Tack on an extra few hours or an extra night to debrief and plan how to use what you've learned.

You may even choose to do a marriage conference on your own. Dave and Claudia Arp recommend a weekend agreement to get the most out of your time away. Here's an example of one of theirs: "We agree to leave work, worries, and other cares at home, realizing they won't go away and will patiently wait for our return. Claudia will compromise and let Dave take the notebook computer along, but with the following restrictions: Dave will not play any new programs…For this weekend, we choose to leave the TV, VCR, and radio unplugged…Claudia agrees to have someone else check our voicemail…For 48 hours we will concentrate on each other, and our goals for the weekend include discussing retirement planning and how to focus and slow down a bit, as well as planning a fun just-for-two vacation for this next year."[5]

We recommend a marriage renewal event at least once a year. When a marriage begins, you enter with a level of relational skills, then year upon year the level of responsibility rises. Each year more responsibility at work, in the community, in the church, and in the family add more and more pressure to a relationship. Most couples make the mistake of thinking the level of relational skill they had upon marriage is enough to carry them through life—nothing could be further from the truth! The best way to stay connected emotionally and to ensure happiness for a lifetime is to build new relational skills into your love year upon year.

Rally the Troops

Sometimes it is impossible to "get away" from the stressors in your life. Travis whistled while he riveted in his final bolts. *Just a few more minutes and I can meet Kelly and the kids at the park for ball practice.* A sudden jerk jolted him out of his daydream. He felt the scaffolding under his feet creak and lurch. He looked down. Below him, three stories down, were dagger-like rebar ends sticking up from the cement floor like stalagmites in a cave. The scaffolding creaked once more, then he felt himself plummeting to the ground.

This is going to be bad. Help, God! Then everything went black.

Travis awoke in the hospital to the faces of emergency technicians and doctors trying to save his life.

"It feels like a sharp knife is in my back. Did one of those rebar ends stab me?"

"Luckily, no. You fell between them," said a masked face above him. "Mr. Jacobson, you have a very bad back injury, but we think you'll walk again. We're doing everything possible."

Suddenly the lights above him began spinning in circles. He felt sick to his stomach, yet unable to move or speak. He shut his eyes and hoped it was all a bad dream.

"Mr. Jacobson. Good news. You should be able to walk. In fact, we'd like to see you try today. But your back has suffered extensive trauma, and you will never be able to work in the construction field again or do any other manual labor."

Sometimes, in the space of a moment, life turns upside down. The perfect life, the one you have planned down to the detail, is gone. You try denial. You may bargain with God. You may be angry or frustrated, but none of those feelings change the circumstances that altered the course of your life. When plan A isn't an option—then what? How can you hold a marriage together when life's circumstances are pulling you apart? Notice how Travis and Kelly managed the stress that was thrust upon them by Travis' accident.

Live in Hope, Not Denial

"When Travis fell, I was in denial. The doctors talked about surgery, so I thought it would be the magic cure. Surgery would be the answer to our problem. I saw the fall as a temporary setback. Travis would be back to normal in a few months, and we could go on with life. I really wanted it to be the answer. We had three kids, two in preschool. And I was only a part-time preschool teacher. You can't live on that!

"Travis had a series of operations, and two years later the reality of it all hit. I had a full-time job and Travis just had another operation. I was pregnant with our fourth, and it was almost Christmas. I thought we'd have a cozy little holiday. I figured things would be tight, but we'd be over this obstacle holding back our lives," Kelly explained.

"That's when we got the news that my surgery had failed."

"The news was devastating."

"But not as devastating as almost losing you," Travis added with tears in his eyes. "That same week, Kelly lost the baby and she really bled. The doctors thought they were losing her. I was scared! Really scared! But she came through."

"I wasn't coping well," Kelly explained. "I was constantly fighting depression. I had supportive family and friends, but I still felt isolated. No one could change what was going on. It was compounded disappointment."

"I was fighting it too," Travis explained. "When the surgery didn't work, I felt something must be wrong with me as a person."

"But something happened in our hearts. Though we didn't have any money, our family and our church brought over gifts and food. We were overwhelmed with the love. A tiny crack of hope came through. It wasn't denial—like we'd wake up and everything would be back the way it was before. It was hope, that we'd somehow get through it." Kelly smiled as the memories rolled out.

"I rededicated my life to Christ. I knew God loved me and my family, and somehow he'd work it out. That was a new feeling for me," Travis added.

"That was one of our favorite Christmas memories. We recommitted ourselves to each other and our marriage. There was renewal there under the tiny twinkling tree lights. It was a new beginning. Instead of focusing on what we didn't have, we began to focus on what we did have. We had each other."

Live in Today, Not Tomorrow

"I had another series of surgeries."

"And then the court battles began. No one wanted to cover his disability. We had several insurance policies, and they all denied their responsibility for coverage. Money was even tighter! And the frustration was compounded by the inhumane treatment by those in the system."

"I really credit Kelly. She hung in there. She loved me. Not for what I could or couldn't do—just for me."

"I knew I had to live today. I could keep hope for tomorrow but I had to live today. For me, a lot of strength came in the investment I'd already put into the relationship. It's a tenacity that says, 'Nothing is going to separate us!' It is stubborn love. Seeing the best in the person and not letting the lies of Satan get a foothold on your heart and mind."

"We had to clearly communicate our expectations, then work with those expectations. We had to live even amidst the bad circumstances. We wanted to build, not tear down, during this time. We had no idea how long it was going to last! You have to make the best of the circumstances. You either make the best of it or it will destroy you. It is a decision. A choice," Travis emphasized.

Live in the New Role

"By far, the toughest factor in the accident and disability was the role reversal that was forced upon us," Kelly noted.

"I was used to hard physical labor," said Travis. "I used to be able to see the fruit of my labor. I built things! I could point to something and say, 'I helped create that.' People valued my work. All of a sudden I was home. I really feel for the mom-at-home. Society doesn't value her work. And the work doesn't stay done!!"

"I missed the kids. I had to find a new way to relate with them," said Kelly. "And I often laugh because now my friends call Travis for his recipes! Seriously, to other couples going through this, I'd say, 'Keep things in perspective.' The danger in role reversal and this kind of family trauma is that you two can grow apart. Women who feel pushed out of the home can get caught up in a career. You can easily create two separate lives under the same roof. You have to be really, really supportive of one another, whatever the contribution is."

"Get people around that are for you and your relationship," adds Travis. "And be humble. Accept and be grateful for what your wife, or others, do for you."

"Be willing to fight for your relationship," Kelly boldly interjected. "Fight for each other and with each other—that's hard to say—but the thing that hurts the most is sidestepping issues. I had to learn it was okay to disagree and keep a discussion going because life doesn't always give easy answers.

"Sometimes, you need outside intervention when the tough times hit. Counseling really helped us. We sought professional help with a counselor and our pastor, and we also spent a lot of time with couples who'd made it through rough circumstances."

Live in Reality, Not in Regrets

"If I could give any advice to couples in unexpected circumstances, I'd say build a spiritual life together. Travis and I have taught a home Bible study for many years. Being in the Bible weekly, preparing for the group, was a great way to keep the right perspective on life. Being in ministry helps you keep your perspective outward. Helping other people makes your problems seem less intense. We also keep journals. I keep a log of prayer requests and how God answers. All this has helped us have compassion. Our kids weren't spoiled, but they have gotten to do wonderful things with their school and ministry and travel. God always provided. God has done amazing things even in our circumstances.

"We're thinking about renewing our vows. We really are two different people from the ones that were married nearly 20 years ago. We've fallen in love all over again."

Stress will most certainly be an active part of your life together, but stress does not need to be devoid of hope. If you provide ample opportunities for discussion and time spent in easy boxes, you will discover that everything in your life can bring you closer to each other.

Consider these musings about the different ways men and women approach life.

Nicknames:
If Laura, Suzanne, Debra, and Rose go out for lunch, they will call each other Laura, Suzanne, Debra, and Rose. But if Mike, Charlie, Bob, and John go out, they will affectionately refer to each other as Fat Boy, Godzilla, Peanut-Head, and Useless.

Eating Out:
When the bill arrives, Mike, Charlie, Bob, and John will each throw in $20.00, even though it's only for $22.50. None of them will have anything smaller, and none will actually admit they want change back.

When the girls get their bill, out come the pocket calculators.

Money:
A man will pay $2 for a $1 item he wants.

A woman will pay $1 for a $2 item she doesn't want.

Bathrooms:
A man has six items in his bathroom: a toothbrush, toothpaste, shaving cream, razor, a bar of soap, and a towel from the Holiday Inn. The average number of items in the typical woman's

bathroom is 337. A man would not be able to identify most of these items.

Arguments:

A woman has the last word in any argument. Anything a man says after that is the beginning of a new argument.

Dressing Up:

A woman will dress up to go shopping, water the plants, empty the garbage, answer the phone, read a book, or get the mail. A man will dress up for weddings and funerals.

Offspring:

Ah, children. A woman knows all about her children. She knows about dentist appointments and romances, best friends and favorite foods, secret fears and hopes and dreams. A man is vaguely aware of some short people living in the house.[6]

4

Waffles and Spaghetti in Love

Preparing for the Main Course

"They say a person needs three things to be truly happy in this world: someone to love, something to do, and something to hope for."

—Thomas Edward Bodett

It was a surprise. Over dinner one night, in casual conversation, matching schedules—as usual because we always have to hunt for moments to steal away and be together—he said he was going to have to go to a convention for work. My heart sank. *Away again*, I thought. Just thinking it made me miss him. I felt like I was always having to share him. He noticed the change in my countenance and muttered something like, "It's only a few days," and stroked my hair reassuringly. I nodded knowingly, and said, "It's just that we get so little time alone."

The next morning, after I knew he'd left the house for work and started his day's appointments, I called his office. I can't remember just what I said to get the information, but I acquired the name of the hotel where he would be staying for the convention. Then I made a call and begged a friend to come stay with the kids.

The day was a flurry. I packed a picnic basket with candles, chocolate, two glasses and a bottle of sparkling drink that had a big bow on it. I remember it well because the bow covered the very small thing I packed to wear later that night. I grabbed a portable stereo and bought a new Kenny G cassette. *He loves jazz,* I wistfully recalled. I threw in my makeup bag—and a toothbrush.

On the way out of town I stopped at the mall. *A new outfit,* I thought. *A night like this needs a new outfit. Something he'll remember. Something that will stop him in his tracks and make him smile at me with that look—that look that makes me melt. It has to be soft, and a good color—and it has to make me feel—well, great!* After several attempts I slipped a long azul sweater over tight black leggings—and I knew I'd found it! I longed for his touch.

Back in the car, I listened to love songs on the radio. The station seemed to play all the songs we'd ever danced to—or sang to each other in whispered tones under soft lights. I found that I was leaning more and more forward in my seat, as if my heart was being drawn to him. The lights from the oncoming cars on the freeway seemed to dance and flicker. It was probably just a normal commute to most but not to me. Tonight was going to be special—a secret rendezvous, a liaison. My heart raced as the odometer clicked down the miles. As I turned on the exit ramp, I felt my heart pounding. My desire for him was becoming so strong I thought I could hear my own heart beat—just like I had heard his so often after we'd been together intimately. I loved to lay quietly in his arms and rest my head on his chest. I breathed deeply and felt as if I could smell the deliciously familiar fragrance of his aftershave.

I parked the car discreetly behind a nearby building. His business partners and associates were also at this conference, and I couldn't take any chances at being seen or having my car recognized. I looked at my watch and sighed in relief. I had timed it just right. They would still be out at the banquet, so I'd have time to sneak into his room undetected.

I must have seemed a little flustered when I asked for the room number and the key because the desk clerk mumbled, "Oh, I'm sorry, ma'am, the register only has one person registered for that room." A little panicked, I managed to pull myself together and answered as confidently as I could, "Oh, I'm his wife and he really wasn't sure if I'd be able to get off work to come." He nodded his head as though he believed me and handed me the key.

I quickly walked across the parking lot, my arms full of the packages of a woman in love. Again, I glanced at my watch. *I'll have to hurry to get everything set up. I want the atmosphere just right when he steps into the room.*

It was perfect. Soft flickering candlelight danced across the ceiling to the mellow sound of a smooth saxophone as he stepped into the room. He saw me standing in the shadows. He stared at me in stunned amazement. I knew at that moment I had recaptured his heart. As I ran to him, he wrapped his arms around me, twirled me around and whispered, "Wow! What a surprise. I'm so glad you've come." Then we kissed and danced and did all the things I had dreamed we'd do. Finally, we fell asleep in each other's arms. My long blonde hair fell across his chest and it all felt so good—so right—and I could hear the beat of his heart as I lay there.

The quiet beeping of my watch alarm was an unwelcome sound the next morning. I knew I had to go but I didn't want to.

Why can't these moments last forever? I quietly slipped into my clothes and gathered up the staples of romance I had brought with me. I ran my fingers through his hair and we kissed. He thanked me again for coming, and he smiled that smile as I closed the door behind me. As I drove out of the parking lot, the sun was peaking up from its slumber and a hint of sunlight spilled across the steering wheel. It caught a corner of one of the facets of my diamond ring—the ring my husband had given me 15 years before. I smiled. *No guilt,* I thought. *Just an affair to remember. An affair with my beloved husband.*

Bill and I still refer to this night as "The Affair." I met a romantic need in Bill by surprising him at the conference. I inserted one of his all-time favorite boxes into one of his least favorite—being one of the few waffles at a conference full of spaghetti!

Romance to Her

Romance to women is when the man in her life ties different aspects of her life together. For example, if Bill calls me up on Tuesday and asks me to go out on Friday, on Wednesday I will get a card in the mail saying, "Can't wait 'til the weekend!" On Thursday, he asks me to wear the cute little black dress he just loves. Then Friday, flowers are delivered with a card, "see ya soon!" and he picks me up and takes me to places I have told him I wanted to go, and we do things I have said I wanted to do. And at the restaurant, there is a gift—already in place—and then on Monday, I get a card in the mail that says, "Thanks for a great evening!" Wow! I am swept off my feet! (He gets bonus points if he arranged child care!) He has tied nearly a week together into a romantic memory. Guys, the good news is that if you take the time to tie many romantic details together like this, the aura of it can last YEARS!

One friend of ours has found a way to give practical items, like toasters and can openers to his wife and not get in trouble over it! The key, tie it to romance. Paul gives his wife, Gail, a practical item every month on their anniversary—and he's done it for over 10 years because he tells her, "I want to give you things I know you will use, because when you use them, you'll be reminded of how much I love you!" But it will work only if you give these items *every* month. You don't want to give your wife a vacuum for an anniversary present unless you want it to be your last anniversary!

Romance to Him

Romancing men is pretty simple. Have clear, simple expectations and stick to them! If we say we're going to dinner and a movie, then we need to stick to that. Don't think that your husband should just *know* that you want to walk on the beach after and talk about hopes and dreams. To really romance a guy, connect some of his favorite easy boxes. For example, if I want to romance Bill, I will get him tickets to a football game, take him to his favorite restaurant, and have great sex when we get home. In fact, he'd give *you* the tickets to the ballgame and skip dinner if he knew for sure there would be sex. Bingo!

Romance is the art of studying each other for the purpose of pleasing one another. Romance is a skill. Guys, if you were athletes—or are athletes—you lifted weights to gain strength. In weight conditioning, you start with lighter weights and then add more repetitions before you add more weight. By repeating exercises (more reps), you gain strength. The same is true with romance. The more you practice it, the stronger you become. The more reps, the more romantic of a lover you will be.

Like any skill, romance can seem awkward in the beginning. Romance is a lot like driving. When you first started to drive, you drove with your hands, both hands, at the 10 and 2 position. But the more you drove, the more comfortable you became. Now you can drive with one hand while eating a Big Mac, tuning your radio, and talking on your cell phone. Romance is one of the basic skills of love. In basketball, when you break the game down, the fundamentals are simply dribble, pass, and shoot—easy, right? Well, not at first, but if you dribble, pass, and shoot long enough, doing the basics frees you to be more creative in a game—it builds confidence. The more you practice romance, the more romantic you are!

Take an RQ Test

Romance is *knowing* your lover. Different personalities prefer different types of romance. What happens is that we expect our mate to love to be loved the way we feel loved. So what's romantic to us is supposed to be romantic to them, right? Wrong!

Many personality tests exist that describe four personality types. We've laid out what expresses love to each of the personality types. Take this RQ (Romantic Quotient) test. But this is an open book exam! See if you can pick yourself out—and see if you can discern which type of lover you are married to.

Type 1 Lover[1]
Knight in Shining Armor; Queen of Hearts

Examples: Lancelot, James Bond, Robin Hood, Crocodile Dundee, Joan of Arc, and Lois Lane

Characteristics:

Dominant
Task-oriented
Extroverted
Loves new experiences
Controling
Focused
Active
Cooperative
Makes a decision and gets on with it
Conquering

Preferences in Romance:

1. Adventurous activity (if in charge)
2. Club Med
3. No guided tours
4. Hiking
5. Anything they decide is a good idea

(Personality Type: Choleric; Dominant; Lion)

Type 2 Lover
The Hopeless Romantic

Examples: Anne of Avonlea, Cupid

Characteristics:

People-oriented
Extroverted
Is the center of attention
Loves to be with lots of people
Enjoys new experiences
Fun
Unique
Exotic
Daring
Looks for new adventures
Active

Preferences in Romance:

1. Anything new
2. Entertainment that is personal and touches the heart
3. Human drama (plays, musicals, concerts, sporting events)
4. Adventurous outings
5. Exotic getaways

(Personality type: Sanguine; Inspirational; Otter)

Type 3 Lover
Wind Beneath My Wings

Examples: Superman, Robert and Elizabeth Browning

Characteristics:

People-oriented
Introverted
Relaxed
Easygoing
Takes it as it comes
Stress free
Has time to talk

Preferences in Romance:

1. Light schedule
2. Simple activities
3. Time to relax
4. Escape from reality flexible
5. Entertainment where there is plenty of time to enjoy it

(Personality Type: Phlegmatic; Steady; Retriever)

Type 4 Lover
True Blue Lover

Examples: Jane Eyre, Romeo and Juliet

Characteristics:

Task-oriented
Introverted
Predictable
Scheduled
Enjoys things that are significant

Preferences in Romance:

1. Guided tours
2. Educational outings
3. Museums
4. Historical tours
5. Long conversations

(Personality Type: Melancholy; Cautious; Beaver)

The Gift of Romance

Both men and women love receiving gifts—those precious momentos of affection. However, buying just the perfect gift can be a challenge—but not if you have Cliffs Notes! And there are Cliffs Notes all around. Try these ideas to find out some clues about what a romantic gift would be for your love:

• Ask his or her friends.

• Look through his or her magazines or catalogs—are there any dog-eared pages?

• Pay attention to what commercials they comment about on TV or radio.

Add Some Zip to Your Do Da (Spice It Up!)

Can your marriage continue to sizzle like it did when you were dating? How can you add a little zip to your love life? You can continue dating throughout your lives. However, couples often complain that life and love become mundane and routine with each passing year. They don't have to! Try these relationship enhancers to put the spark back in your love life.

Look back. Try a date that revisits some of those early memories of your life together. Take a trip to the place you first met, first kissed, or where your marriage proposal took place. If finances or distance are a concern, plan a picnic and bring a photo album of the early years and reminisce. Put on "your" song in the stereo and take a drive to your old neighborhood, high school or college, or favorite restaurant. Maybe this is the year to renew your vows or write new vows for the next decade of life ahead. Looking back can help reestablish those feelings that first drew you together, and it can remind you both of all the years of memories you have invested in each other.

Look ahead. Each of us keeps a list of "dream dates" that we'd like to go on. Once a year Bill and I remake the list and give it to each other as a "gift." We also give each other a "love list" of at least ten things that cost nothing but make us feel loved. Having these lists helps us surprise one another on a regular basis. By looking ahead you can also invest in your marriage by attending a marriage seminar, conference, or retreat. You may also choose to invest in your relationship by purchasing a gift that says, "I love the person you are becoming. I'm excited about your life— and ours. Just wanted you to know I believe in your dream." When a couple will invest in one another's dreams and plan for the transitions of life, they gain the ability to fall in love over and over again.

Seize the moment. Invest in the now. Practice the art of touch. Reach over and hold a hand, give a squeeze, pat a back. With all the technology available today, there are plenty of ways to reach out and touch the one you love. Leave a message on voicemail, fax a love note, or e-mail a missive that is filled with symbols and word pictures that only you two will understand. Try something radical—stop by home or your spouse's work just to whisper, "I love you" and then drop a single rose on the desk as you leave. Or call your mate and read a few verses from the Song of Solomon over the phone.

Romance doesn't have to take a lot of money, just a little bit of time spent thinking about your mate. After all, the gift your spouse most enjoys is you!

Encouragement Can Be Romantic

You can do a lot to encourage creativity in your mate. Trust and emotional safety build creativity. Over the next few days, listen for an area of insecurity in your spouse. Maybe she is a little anxious about her weight—or he is a little melancholy over his fading youth. Make a list of ways you can "praise" or encourage the one you love in that area of concern. Then prepare a "gift of praise" designed to encourage. It could be something you say, something you do, or a tangible gift. The key is to focus on the one you love—not focus on what society, the media, or your next-door neighbor says romance is!

Don't Forget to Focus

On those rare days when life is a bit slower, it is easy for me (Pam) to long for and pursue Bill because I have spent time quietly admiring him. On other, more hectic days, I have to choose to focus my distracted thoughts on him and my desire to be with him.

I have to plan to remember Bill romantically. His picture is on my key chain. I might give a quick "I love you" call to his office. When changing my clothes I might pull a suit out of his closet just to smell the remaining fragrance of his cologne. I keep the cards he's given me handy so I can reread one or two. But by far, the best way to prepare my heart to enjoy Bill is to take a quiet minute in the car or at my desk, close my eyes, and remember one of our special intimate moments. Choosing to set aside my distractions and focusing my thoughts on him draws my heart to his.

I (Bill) have to choose to focus on Pam as well. I keep many pictures of her in my office. I call home regularly throughout the day—sometimes just to hear her voice on the answering machine! I shut my eyes and remember past times together. I periodically like to go shopping for her. Buying her something romantic or sexy keeps my heart longing to be with her. And I keep a list of things I can do that Pam loves with me at all times.

Make a List—Check It Twice

To discover what is romantic to each of you, try these exercises:

1. Each of you make a list of ten free things that the one you love can do for you that makes you feel more loved. It can be anything—sometimes the obvious, like: "Say 'I love you,'" or the not so obvious, "Take out the trash without having to be asked!" Make a date to exchange lists and talk about why you chose your ten items—that is where you'll really gain some insight on what is romantic to the one you love. For example, since we've been married, on my (Pam's) list is, "Run a bubble bath for me, create candlelight, then come sit and talk with me, maybe even massage my back." This way I am assured of Bill's undivided attention, and I get a quiet, uninterrupted niche of time carved out of a hectic schedule. When we were dating, my list included things like: Come visit me at work, go on a walk, or take me to the beach at sunset.

2. Make a list of "Dream Dates." If money were no object, what ten dates would each of you like to go on this year? You may get some great birthday or anniversary ideas out of this one. Maybe you can't afford Hawaii—but possibly some island music, some passion fruit and guava juice, and theater tickets to "South Pacific" might be within reach. Again, ask the one you love why these dates are romantic to him or her. They may or may not know. It could just be they are different than the movie-dinner rut! To change the rut you may need to change the mood.

List ten things that speak love to your heart that are free. (For example, I think it is romantic when Bill takes out the trash or puts gas in my car for me. Bill thinks it is romantic if I sit and watch a football game with him, all cuddled up next to him— and I am even more romantic if I actually watch the game (and not read a book!) and interact with him with, "Do you think Brock will ever throw like that QB?"

Ten Free Things That Express Love to Me

His
   1.
   2.
   3.
   4.
   5.
   6.
   7.
   8.
   9.
   10.

Hers
   1.
   2.
   3.
   4.
   5.
   6.
   7.
   8.
   9.
   10.

If money was no object, (we know it is) and you could go on a romantic date anywhere and it would be paid for by a third party, list ten dream dates you'd like to go on:

Ten Dream Dates

His

1.

2.

3.

4.

5.

6.

7.

8.

9.

10.

Hers

1.

2.

3.

4.

5.

6.

7.

8.

9.

10.

Copy these lists and keep them where you can find them, and you'll have the information to pass the romance test!

How to Set the Mood

Create anticipation. Send roses to your sweetheart with a note saying how anxious you are to be with her. Call your loved one on the phone and leave a message on voicemail of how much you long to be with her. (Be careful that it is voicemail—not an answering machine—you don't know who might be listening to a message machine!) Send a card each day for a month, two weeks, or even one week prior to a big vacation or anniversary.

Buy a new outfit, new cologne or perfume—or better yet, wrap up one of these items, or something even more personal, and deliver it with a note that again proclaims your desperate yearning to be with your love.

Create a plan. Think out your special date or getaway. Try to plan ahead and pack the items that would make life easier once you get there. For example, call ahead to the bed-and-breakfast you are staying at and check to see if they pack picnic baskets, or if they have the basket and you'll need the supplies.

Think of the small touches. If you take a midnight picnic to the beach for a fire and a snuggle under the moonlight, bring a warm blanket or sleeping bags, firewood, matches, and kindling or newspaper to start the fire. You'll most likely remember your guitar or a tape player and music—but don't forget towels and some extra water to wash off your sandy feet in case you decide to go in the water.

Even if your date is at home while the kids are away, if you plan ahead you can create a mood by walking the steps your spouse will walk as he or she enters the house. Place a note or small gift on the front doorstep, sprinkle a path of hearts, Valentines or rose petals to create a walkway to the dining room. You can also create a path using luminarias (bags filled with sand and a small candle) or candles or balloons. Use your imagination. A variation of this theme is to place notes with clues leading the person to you, to a gift, or to a romantic setting—like dinner on the roof.

You could choose a few poems from a poetry book to read aloud—or better yet, write one! Plan topics of discussion or romantic questions for conversation starters.

Try a few of these questions to fan the flame on your love life:

1. If someone were to write a book about our love, what would you title it?

2. If I put my hands over your eyes and said, "Surprise!" what would you want to see when you opened your eyes?

3. If we were to rendezvous anyplace on earth, where would you want to go and why?

4. What kind of car describes me best?

5. What's been the nicest surprise of being married to me?

Create a sensory experience. Smell—Using your five senses, prepare the setting. How can you make it smell beautiful? Try scented candles, potpourri in a bowl, fresh flowers, a scent ring placed on a light bulb, or potpourri burners. Another great smell is that of a great meal. Bake some cookies, fresh bread, brownies, or a gourmet meal! Then make sure you smell terrific too! On a trip to the Hawaiian islands, we stocked up on cocoa butter tanning sticks just because we loved the smell!

Sight—Scan the surroundings. Is it clean? Things don't have to be perfect—just comfortable. Everything always looks better in soft lighting. Decorate a room with candles, invest in sconces for your walls or hurricane lamps for the dresser. Tiny white Christmas lights make a great addition to any setting. Weave a few strands of lights on a tree, or string them on your ceiling to create that "starry night" effect.

In daylight, plants and fresh flowers go a long way in creating a romantic setting, as do lots of pillows and fresh white linen with china and crystal. If you can't create the setting, go to a romantic lake, beach, mountain resort, garden, or fine restaurant for at least a portion of the date.

Taste—Try a variety of palate pleasers. Set out a bowl of fresh strawberries, fine chocolates, or a plate of petit fours. The best option is always try to include something you know your sweetheart loves. If I (Bill) want to cheer Pam up, I'm sure to have a hit by ordering some Dewar's Chews—a fun tasty taffy from Pam's hometown in Bakersfield, California. By having some chews on hand, I tell her I have been thinking of her. This gift always impresses her because I have to order them.

Sound—Invest in romantic music. This one is really personal choice! It's great if you both like the same kind of music. If that isn't a possibility, then try something completely different than normal. For example, if she loves country and you love rock 'n' roll, then go for jazz or classical music playing very softly in the background. Or get ethnic and play music from the islands, from Africa, or somewhere exotic!

A wonderful option is positive romantic music. Look for lyrics that promote commitment, sacrifice, and sensitivity. Let the lyrics build into your relationship as you relax together. If you are married, these songs are a welcome break from the "You cheated on me so I'm going to get drunk or get even" blue kind of songs.

Touch—Our skin covers our whole body so it makes sense to consider what might feel nice next to the skin. This is why romantic settings often include water, Jacuzzi, swimming, massage, lotion, satin, silk, and velvet. We often choose clothes that feel good next to our skin—but consider also how the fabric feels on the outside. Bill has some sweaters that are scratchy and itchy while others are soft and invite me into his arms.

Be creative and you'll find it easy to stay heart to heart.

Diamonds may very well be a girl's best friend, but romance doesn't have to cost to be romantic. The best gift is the gift of investing yourself and your time in the romantic encounter. Here's a list to spark some of your own creative juices:

25 Free or Nearly Free Ideas for Great Dates

1. Have a candlelit picnic in an unusual location, like your rooftop, a park bench, or overlooking the ocean.

2. Go on a photo date where you snap pictures of each other all over the city. If finances permit it, take them to a one-hour developing location. You may want to frame your favorite and give it to your spouse with a note. The others can be sent as postcards to each other all through the year.

3. Walk or bicycle to an inexpensive ice cream shop or a fancy coffeehouse.

4. Drive in the mountains, arriving in time for a sunset or moonlit stroll.

5. Go to a park, push one another in the swings, and talk. Take turns listing A to Z the reasons you love your mate.

6. Walk the mall. The goal is not to buy, but to test perfume and cologne along the way.

7. Have a squirt gun fight.

8. Write clues on dime-store Valentines and place them around town, then take your love on a car rally or treasure hunt. The date consists of gathering clues and small romantic treasures like poems, chocolates, and other small treats.

9. Go to the library and check out a poetry book.

10. Write a song or a poem and perform it for the one you love. Even an original version of "Roses are Red..." can be a treasure when it's from the heart.

11. Reenact a portion of a timeless romantic drama. Shakespeare's *Romeo and Juliet* is a great place to begin.

12. Celebrate your married romance. Spend the day in bed. Prepare ahead and have breakfast in bed. Bring piles of magazines and play soft music. Rest in your love.

13. Reminisce over old photo albums or your wedding album. Set the mood by relaxing together and talking by firelight or candlelight. Another option is to have your children play waiter and waitress and serve a romantic dinner, then tell them the story of how you fell in love. After they are in bed, choose one other idea on this list to enjoy.

14. Go to a local Christian bookstore and buy a book on marriage and read it together.

15. Have a living room luau. Often local music stores have island music at rock bottom prices.

16. Borrow plants from all your friends and neighbors and turn your patio into a private garden retreat and enjoy a quiet dinner.

17. Rent an old-fashioned romantic movie. The movies made in the '30s through the '50s are a good place to start.

18. Rob the kids' toy chests. Go fly a kite or play some one-on-one basketball.

19. Work out together. Go for a jog, do aerobics to a video, or visit a gym.

20. Bake something extravagant together. Bonus points if you *both* help in the clean up.

21. Play a board game together. Classics like Scrabble or the Ungame are good conversation starters.

22. Put on your special song and waltz around the living room.

23. Play 20 questions. Each of you think of ten questions you'd love to know the answer to. Try questions like, "If you introduced me to a stranger today, what one thing would you say I do that you *really* appreciate about me?" or "If money was not a factor, where would you like to go on a romantic getaway?"

24. Anticipate the future. All marriages go through seasons. Consider buying a book to help prepare for the next season of love.

25. Renew your vows (or write personal vows, if you didn't do that in your original ceremony). This can be a private affair or you can invite the children or friends and celebrate.

Remember, it's not the expense of the gift but the thought that counts!

5

Waffles and Spaghetti in the Bedroom

Sugar and Spice

"Marrying for love is a bit risky, but it is so honest God can't help but smile on it!"

—Josh Billings

On a transatlantic flight, a plane passes through a severe storm. The turbulence is awful, and things go from bad to worse when one wing is struck by lightning. One woman loses it. She stands up in the front of the plane and screams, "I'm too young to die!" Twice more she wails, "I'm too young to die! I'm too young to die!"

She shakes and sobs for just a moment, and then gathers her courage and continues, "Well, if I'm going to die I want my last minutes on earth to be memorable! I've had plenty of sex in my life, but no one has ever made me really feel like a woman! Well,

I've HAD IT! Is there ANYONE on this plane who can make me feel like a WOMAN?"

For a moment there is silence. All the passengers have forgotten their own peril, and they all stare, riveted, at the desperate woman in the front of the plane. Then a man stands up in the rear of the plane.

"I can make you feel like a woman."

He's gorgeous: Tall, well-built, with flowing black hair and dark blue eyes. He starts to walk slowly up the aisle, unbuttoning his shirt one button at a time. No one moves. The woman is breathing heavily in anticipation as the strange man approaches. He removes his shirt. Her lips part slightly. Muscles ripple across his chest as he reaches the trembling woman and extends his arm and holds his shirt out and whispers...

"Iron this."[1]

Perplexing Passion

Sex is one of the greatest, yet most awkward, activities that husbands and wives engage in. A successful sexual encounter will leave a man and his wife relaxed, satisfied, and thrilled to be in love. A couple who is in sync with each other sexually will be more confident, will think clearer, and will be more willing to sacrifice themselves for the good of the relationship. The sad fact, though, is that few couples experience a satisfying sexual relationship on a regular basis.

To be sure, this is a complex and highly emotional issue, but there is hope that every couple can gain enough insight into the sexual dance of marriage to have a long-term, fulfilling intimate life. The keys to great sex are accepting that men and women are different sexually, valuing your spouse's sexual response as much as you value your own, and committing yourself to the behaviors that meet your spouse's sexual needs.

If Only You Could Know What I Know

Men and women approach sex differently, and there is nothing you can do to change that. Most men would like their wives to be more aggressive in their intimate encounters and most women would like their husbands to slow down and be more understanding of their emotional needs. This tension exists because husbands and wives have been wired differently by their Creator in the realm of sexual pleasure.

Men, your wife's sexual fulfillment is connected to everything else in her life. When she feels close to you emotionally, she is more responsive. When she is in touch with her children and she is proud of how you father them, she is more attracted to you. When her career is moving forward and you are supportive of her pursuits, she finds you more irresistible than you already are. The more you are a part of her life, the stronger her desire for you is.

Every month she is reminded of her reproductive potential as she goes through her menstrual cycle. As a man, you would probably like to think that her constant interaction with her reproductive process would make her more interested in sex. But much of her menstrual cycle is uncomfortable and inconvenient. She has no choice but to experience this cycle every month. Some days, she feels very sexy and interested in intimate contact with you. On other days, she is out of sorts even though she tries not to be.

Four different hormones are involved in a woman's reproductive cycle, influencing her behavior and how she feels at different times of the month. Almost all doctors accept that a significant number of women suffer regularly from a variety of physical ailments commonly called PMS (Pre-Menstrual Syndrome). PMS has six major physical symptoms and ten mental ones. Among these are irritability, depression, anxiety, hostility, headaches, and backache as well as unusually painful menstruation. This is a drastic list, and it is hard to feel sexy when you are battling with these challenges. Fortunately, most sufferers will experience no more than three of them during any one cycle.[2]

So what does this mean to the average woman? Do we use PMS as an excuse to get us out of work, sex, housework, or pumping our own gas? Well, we can't go that far since "at the 1976 Olympics an American swimmer won three gold medals and broke a world record while at the height of her period. And so far as pregnancy is concerned, the Russians revealed after the 1964 Games that no fewer than ten of their twenty-six female champions were pregnant when they earned their medals!"[3] I (Pam) have to admit I have toyed with the idea that since PMS is followed by menses, maybe I should have the right to be pathetic for 10-14 days each month. The only problem is I don't want to be pathetic half my life! I could legitimately croon the line, "Not tonight, I have a headache," except that early in my marriage I discovered a magazine article in my OB-GYN's office that claimed sex actually helps a headache go away! A short while later, I read another article that claimed sex helped alleviate the symptoms of PMS and menstrual cramps. Now, I know what you're thinking—my OB-GYN must be a guy who filled his office with propaganda. Well, no, she was a wonderful woman doctor!

I don't want to give the impression that good sex is the answer to all your PMS troubles, but no sex is not the answer either. After the birth of our second child, Bill noticed that I seemed to have a pattern of some negative emotions. I regularly became irritable, panicked, bossy, and cynical. On those days Bill could do no right and the world seemed like it was on the edge of impending doom. I either tried to control everything around me by barking out orders or I fell into a mild depression—wanting to stay in my pajamas, watch old movies, and eat chocolate. Bill began to mark these mood swings on his calendar at work. After about three months, he brought the calendar home.

"Honey, I have some dates on the calendar you might be interested in seeing."

"Really?" I asked curiously.

"Yes. You said you don't feel like yourself since Zachery was born. Well, I think it is worse for you on certain days of the month. The past few months I have been marking down the days that seem especially hard for you, and, Pam, it seems that day 21 of your cycle is the worst day of the month for you. That's the day that everything seems wrong. You cry more, get angry easier, and feel like staying in bed. All those things that are bothering you seem to be worse on day 21 of your cycle."

Because it was *not* day 21 of my cycle, I was impressed he cared enough to keep track of this. I began to note these days on my own calendar. I planned a lighter schedule on days 20, 21, and 22. I tried not to make snap decisions or judgments on those days. I set aside time to exercise and rest more on those days. Shortly after that, I took a women's studies course, and we were required to write in a daily journal how we were feeling physically, emotionally, and sexually. I noticed all kinds of patterns in my life based upon my menstrual cycle. There were difficult days nagged by headaches and cramps but there were also great days when I felt strong and sexy!

Regarding sexuality, though the news on PMS may be discouraging, there is a remarkable benefit to the way in which women are created. It takes more for her to reach arousal, but when things are right she can experience pleasure much longer and more intensely than her husband. The big difference between male and female orgasm is that a woman does not necessarily need to recover from one orgasm before she can have another. "Many women…frequently experience two or more orgasms in a row without descending from the plateau phase of sexual arousal. It is very possible that most women can experience multiple orgasms, but do not do so for lack of experimentation or because of psychological or social inhibition."[4]

It is obvious from female anatomy God intended that sexual pleasure would be a normal part of a woman's life. "This is not in the least surprising since the interior of the vagina—though equipped with muscles admirably suited for the task of providing a man with sexual satisfaction—is a comparatively insensitive area of the body. The clitoris, on the other hand, is the only organ in the animal kingdom which has the sole function of giving its owner sexual pleasure. Though small, it contains as many nerve endings as a penis."[5] When a man commits himself to his wife's sexual fulfillment a fascinating dynamic takes place. She will experience orgasms more often and may enjoy multiple orgasms on many occasions. He, on the other hand, will have his ego boosted because he feels like a better lover with each orgasm she experiences.

Sex in the Box

It has been said that sex is all men think about. This may be more true than any of us want to admit, but it doesn't mean that all men are warped in their sexual activity. Sex is a different pursuit for men than women because of the way they are made. The simplest way to understand a man's sex drive is to picture it in the center box of his waffle. As we have mentioned before, it is bigger than any of the others and can be entered from any other box. The reason this box is bigger is that it has compartments in it. Since men are focused on sex much more than women, it is easy to conclude they have a single-minded approach to sexual activity. But in reality, there are three independent forces that drive a man's desire: a reproductive mandate, sexual tension, and intimacy.

Reproductive mandate: God created mankind for survival. To ensure its success, God built into the human species characteristics that constantly encourage sexual activity. In the case of men, God gave them eyes to see. It is generally understood that men are visually stimulated. When an attractive woman is in the vicinity, a man will notice her instinctively. It has been this way from the beginning of creation. When God created Eve, Adam was so taken by her appearance that he spontaneously broke out in song.

> This is now bone of my bones
>   and flesh of my flesh;
> she shall be called "woman,"
>   for she was taken out of man (Genesis 2:23).

The original plan was to give each man eyes to admire his wife throughout their life together. The intensity of a man's ability to notice women was given to him so his wife would be attractive to him all the days of his life.

This characteristic of men has been vastly exploited over the years. The beauty industry has put incredible pressure on women to look fantastic. As a man sees more and more artificially beautiful women, he may lose his appreciation for the natural beauty of his wife. His sexual eyes were intended to allow his wife to go through the natural changes that age and motherhood bring without losing her appeal to him. She would continue to look great to him because he could feast his eyes on her. The modern media has turned his concentration into a commodity. As a result, any man who wants to have a lifelong relationship of pleasure with his wife must discipline his eyes to stay focused on her. To accomplish this, and to protect all areas of a man's sexuality, a man must put Jesus in charge of each box, especially this visual box. Job 31:1 says, "I made a covenant with my eyes not to look lustfully at a girl." A man would be wise to take Job's advice.

For those of you who think it is just a matter of maturity, consider the following. Women experience a roller coaster ride in the menstrual cycle because of hormones. Likewise, men experience intensity in their focus because of hormones. "Although many researchers have tried to prove otherwise, there seems to be very little connection between the female sex hormones and sexuality. Oestrogens are involved in lubricating the vagina, but removing a woman's ovaries generally has very little effect on her sexuality."[6] In contrast, "the male sex hormones cannot be dismissed quite so lightly: there is a connection between sexual behavior and androgen levels in both men and women...According to one study, the likelihood of a couple having intercourse at any particular time is at least partly a function of how much testosterone the woman has in her bloodstream: the more she has, the more likely it is."[7] Men think about sex because the testosterone levels in their bloodstream encourage them to do so. In another fascinating study, "when sex offenders are given oestrogens to reduce their sex drive, it seems to be the cognitive aspects of their sexuality, such as the amount of time they spend thinking about sex, which are affected, rather than the physiological aspects—their ability to get an erection, for example."[8]

It seems fair to conclude, then, that men will instinctively notice the beauty of women on a regular basis. This is why the phrase, "It is not the first look that will get you in trouble, it is the second," is so popular. For a husband and wife, this can be a source of irritation if he has wandering eyes, especially when he is with her! But it can also be a source of success. The wife who understands this visual box can enter it at any time by drawing attention to her body. Dancing, wearing lingerie, and slowly undressing in your husband's presence can be powerful magnets that draw his heart toward yours. When you accept that the strong visual orientation of men is something God intended, you can appreciate lists such as this one:

HOW TO IMPRESS A WOMAN: compliment her, cuddle her, kiss her, caress her, love her, stroke her, tease her, comfort her, protect her, hug her, hold her, spend money on her, dine her, buy things for her, listen to her, care for her, stand by her, support her, go to the ends of the earth for her.

HOW TO IMPRESS A MAN: show up naked.[9]

In addition to the frequency with which sexual thoughts occur to the average man, he also has no option but to be aware of the pleasurable reproductive potential of his body. It starts in his developmental years and continues throughout most of his adult life. "With the arrival of puberty, children have their attention drawn to their genitals as a result of…anatomical and hormonal changes…At this point the experiences of the two sexes diverge sharply. When a girl begins to menstruate, she may feel proud to be grown-up at last, but the physical changes she undergoes are not likely to bring her obvious sexual pleasure. A boy, on the other hand, starts to have erotic dreams and frequently finds himself with an unsolicited erection. Like it or not, he can hardly fail to be aware of his genitals or of their potential as a source of pleasure."[10]

Sexual tension: The second compartment of the sex box has to do more with stress than intimacy. Following ejaculation, semen begins to build up in a man's body, creating a sense of physical pressure. When a man becomes sexually active, his body adjusts to an anticipated schedule of intercourse. For example, if a husband and wife start off their relationship enjoying sexual pleasure every couple of days, his body will prepare to ejaculate on that schedule. But no couple ever stays "on schedule," and that is where the tension builds. His body still prepares to release the semen even if he knows intellectually it is unreasonable.

For most men, this is where the tyranny of sex shows up. When he is not able to ejaculate "on schedule," he experiences a number of physiological and emotional reactions. The feeling of pressure in his groin area becomes a nagging reminder. He finds himself staring at his wife more as her features intensify in his mind. He longs to be with her as her features look more attractive to him. As time goes by, he then becomes irritable, even unreasonable. He loses sight of much of what is great about life. Music seems dull, sunsets are distractions, conversation is painful, and all other tasks become either boring or overwhelming. The whole time he is saying to himself, "Get a grip. You are stronger than this. It won't hurt to wait." But no amount of reasoning with himself reduces the tension he feels in his body.

This struggle is intensified more if stress is high in life. The process of orgasm for a man is so intense that it is his preferred method for stress relief. As general stress increases in a man's life, his awareness of the tension in his body is heightened. The release of semen at ejaculation not only relieves the tension in his body, it also transports him mentally and emotionally into the box of sexual expression. When he enters that box, all the cares of his life are put on hold. The fact that good sex is usually followed by sleep only adds to the impact that sexual activity has in relieving stress in his life.

I believe that the average man would like to be able to turn this part of his sex drive off. It is persistent and unyielding. The tension builds involuntarily and consumes much more of his life than he is comfortable with. He also has no idea how to explain this to his wife. He doesn't want her to think he lacks self-control, or worse, that he has a perverted outlook on sex. He also doesn't want to put undue pressure on her, but he can't stop the process going on inside himself. It is rare to hear of a man who has successfully explained this to his wife. Either he hasn't tried because he is convinced she will never understand, or he made an attempt and her reaction was too extreme. Every man longs for his wife to be understanding of this compartment because he is bound to live with it. When she is sensitive and compassionate about the constant intensity of his sex drive, he is amazed and falls in love with her over and over again. When she is critical of it or insensitive, he turns inward and silently fights the struggle alone.

Desire for intimacy. The third compartment of a man's sex box is the one that women find attractive. A man does not love sex just because of what it does physically, he also longs to be significantly connected to the love of his life. He wants to know his wife, and he wants to be known by her. He longs for the safe haven of a loving marriage just as she does. The difference is that men visit this box while his wife weaves intimacy into the fabric of her life. When a man is in the intimacy box, he is attentive to his wife's needs, he is sensitive to her emotions, and he is a patient listener. The biggest complaint we hear from wives is that their husbands don't spend enough time in this box. She wants to be close to him, and she has experienced enough times of intimacy with him to know that he can do it. However, it is often confusing to her why he doesn't spend more time in the pursuit of intimacy.

Without argument, this is frustrating and disappointing to the wife who wants all of their sexual encounters to be expressions of love and intimacy, but the three compartments of a man's sexual desire can be a great source of variety in your sexual interaction as a couple. Because he is vitally aware of the beauty of his wife and wants to explore their sexual potential, he will be willing to lead them into new expressions of their love. Because he experiences consistent tension in his body, some of a couple's interaction will be almost athletic and the focus will be on fun. Because he desires intimacy and emotional connection, some of their sexual encounters will be an extension of the connection they share socially, spiritually, emotionally, and intellectually.

Take Turns

The greatest way you can show your spouse you value his or her sexuality is by committing yourself to learning how to give pleasure rather than take it. Our friends, Jim and Sally Conway, authors of *Traits of a Lasting Marriage*, like to describe the differences between men's and women's sexual response this way: Women respond like an electric stove. You push the button to turn on the burner and there's no immediate response. Slowly the burner warms up until it is red hot. When you turn the burner off, it continues to be red hot and then slowly cools back down. Men, on the other hand, respond like a gas burner—instant on, instant off!

Gary Smalley uses a similar metaphor. He says that women warm up like Crock-Pots while men are like microwaves. Like perfectly timed high-wire performers, there is certainly a rush in experiencing orgasm together, but it isn't the only means for sharing sexual pleasure.

Give the Gift

Simultaneous climax is marvelous, ecstatic, and thrilling, but giving the gift of understanding brings its own form of joy to your relationship. Sacrificing to please your spouse sexually is a mature gift of love. The apostle Paul explains God's picture of true unity:

> Do nothing out of selfish ambition or vain conceit, but
> in humility consider others better than yourselves. Each

of you should look not only to your own interests, but also to the interests of others. Your attitude should be the same as that of Christ Jesus (Philippians 2:3-5).

To be a gift, it has to be willingly given. One of the most often-asked questions we get is, "What is okay? What is permissible and acceptable to God in the area of marital sexuality?" Let's look at a few key verses:

> For this reason a man will leave his father and mother and be united to his wife, and they will become one flesh (Genesis 2:24).

Marriage is between two people, a man and his wife. No one else should be a participant—not in person, in print, or on video. This is why pornography is detrimental to a marriage relationship. It violates the prime directive of sexual love. Sex is between you two alone.

> Marriage should be honored by all, and the marriage bed kept pure, for God will judge the adulterer and all the sexually immoral (Hebrews 13:4).

Sex is designed for married couples. Any sexual activity outside marriage creates complications that will haunt you as individuals for the rest of your life. Extramarital sex does not spice up a marriage, it destroys it from the inside out.

> The husband should fulfill his marital duty to his wife, and likewise the wife to her husband. The wife's body does not belong to her alone but also to her husband. In the same way, the husband's body does not belong to him alone but also to his wife. Do not deprive each other except by mutual consent and for a time, so that you may devote yourselves to prayer. Then come together again so that Satan will not tempt you because of your lack of self-control (1 Corinthians 7:3-5).

You and your spouse were designed to give sexual pleasure to one another. It is interesting that the Bible has very little to say about what is acceptable or unacceptable in the sexual expression of love between a husband and wife. Instead of giving lists, the Bible presents guidelines. First, sexual love is to be given freely. Second, every sexual activity is to be an expression of love. Third, every intimate act is to be done with respect. This implies that you should only do what the two of you agree upon. Your potential is found in the balance between courageously giving yourself to your spouse without ever forcing him or her to do what he or she is unwilling to do.

Foreplay Finesse

Women want a lover with a slow hand and a listening ear. A husband who lovingly talks to his wife and patiently caresses her makes it possible for her to catch up with him in the sexual dance. A man who is in a hurry will frustrate his wife because she is just getting warmed up when he is finished. In the Song of Songs, we meet an insightful young groom who understands his wife's need for a patient lover. To understand the passage, you must know that in the Song, the picture of a garden is used as a symbolic representation for a woman's vagina.

> You are a garden locked up, my sister, my bride;
>   you are a spring enclosed, a sealed fountain.
> Your plants are an orchard of pomegranates
>   with choice fruits,
>   with henna and nard,
>   nard and saffron,
>   calamus and cinnamon,
>   with every kind of incense tree,
>   with myrrh and aloes
>   and all the finest spices.
> You are a garden fountain,

> a well of flowing water
> streaming down from Lebanon (Song of Songs 4:12-15).

Notice that at the beginning of this stanza, the garden is closed. But through the power of his words and caresses (obvious in the context), the garden is flowing freely and fragrantly. Throughout the Song these two lovers experience encounters very similar to this, encouraging each husband to patiently, gently, and completely love his wife.

But this is not all there is to the love life of the king and his bride. She, too, understands that her man is a passionate, virile man with consistent desire for his wife. She has figured out that all it takes to arouse his interest is the sight of her as an available lover. That is why we see in Song 1:4 her willingness to assertively focus on making him glad he married her. "Take me away with you—let us hurry! Let the king bring me into his chambers."

Because we value the differences God has put in our sexual responses, sometimes I (Bill) will say to Pam, "Honey, I have all night—this one's for you." At other times, I (Pam) catch a quick peek at my watch, grab Bill's lapels or his tie, and lead him to the bedroom as I say, "I've got a minute—this one's for you!"

Set Boundaries to Protect Your Love

Bill and I have some pretty tight boundaries that guard our relationships with those of the opposite sex. We are never alone with a person of the opposite sex in a counseling setting. We never dine with those of the opposite sex alone, nor do we travel alone with members of the opposite sex. We even make it a practice of dropping off those of the opposite sex before we take home those of the same sex in a carpool situation. But more important than these structural boundaries, we have emotional boundaries. We do not share with others what our spouse should hear first. In other words, our deepest sorrows and greatest thrills are not shared with anyone until first shared with each other.

But the boundary that protects our love more than any other is the choice to walk away from any relationship in which we are feeling sexual attraction towards another member of the opposite sex—and we tell each other we've made that choice.

For example, I (Pam) was flying home from a long trip, and I was on my last leg when the plane was delayed in takeoff. I sat next to a retired couple, but soon a handsome military officer sat across from me and struck up a conversation. He seemed to want to know all about why I was traveling. Soon he learned I was a writer and a Christian leader. He seemed very interested in my opinions, and he hung on my every word. I was tired and the attention was a welcome relief to the impersonal nature of traveling alone. However, I was careful to stay safely beside the retired couple next to me, drawing them into the conversation at every natural opening. When the officer learned that Bill and I speak on relationships, he began to share all the exotic places he had traveled and the exciting events and places he had taken women to romance them. Finally the plane was ready to board, and I stood up to stand in line, as did the retired couple and the officer. I was sensing that I was enjoying the attention from the handsome officer a little too much and boarding the plane was going to be a welcome exit—until I realized the airline had seated us next to each other.

The officer continued to engage me in conversation. Inside warning bells and whistles were going off in my heart. The Holy Spirit was whispering, *Pam, this is how it starts. You are tired. You are vulnerable. You miss Bill terribly because you've been away from him. You need to move AWAY!* I dismissed myself to go to the rest room and I spotted an empty seat near the back of the plane and returned to my seat to gather my things.

"It was very nice meeting you, however, I have a great deal of work I must accomplish and there's an empty seat. I know you are tired from your long trip, so I thought you might enjoy a little more elbow room yourself." With that, I gathered my things, turned, and left. I dropped my books into the empty seat, went directly to the rest room, and dropped the business card he had given me into the toilet and flushed away the opportunity for any further contact. It felt great to obey God and my conscience. It empowered my love for Bill. I felt a rush of excitement, knowing that I would see my husband again in just a few hours.

I didn't tell Bill right away. I had missed him and he me, so I wanted our first few hours to include a sexually satisfying time together. A few days later, when he and I were feeling very emotionally connected, I shared what had happened on the airplane. I began the conversation with, "Honey, I want to share an emotional experience that shook me up because I love and value our love so much. You are the most wonderful man in the whole world. No one can compare with you and my feelings for you. But on the last trip I took, I saw how easy it would be to fall for flattery, especially when I was so physically tired and, honey, I think our busy lives had me missing your company, connecting with you. I never want to feel that vulnerable again. How can we make sure that even with all my travel I always feel emotionally connected to you?"

I (Bill) discovered the importance of this early in my pastoring career. A woman in our church had asked if I would meet with her to help her work through some of the difficult issues of her past. She had attended enough services to build confidence that I had some insight into her situation. The problem was that she had the same body type as Pam, and she had some of the same mannerisms. I knew that I loved Pam more than anyone on earth, but I could tell I would be emotionally vulnerable if I met with her alone. Rather than just say, "No, I am sorry but I can't do that," I said to her, "If you will ask three of your friends to come in with you to every session, take all your phone calls, and hold you accountable to do your homework, I'll agree."

I figured she would never be able to get three friends to agree to this commitment, so I dismissed the thought of ever meeting with her. Three weeks later, she called and said, "All right, I've got three friends. When do we start?" What happened next was astounding. Because there were close friends of hers there, emotions never wandered. She felt safe to work on the issues of her life, and I felt no temptation to get attached to her. I was simply guiding the ship these four ladies were sailing on. As a result, she grew quicker than anyone I've ever helped and a new plan for helping people was established. I was so impressed with the process that I do all my appointments with females, and most of my appointments with men, this way. When I get home after a day of helping people, my heart is clear to love Pam because she is the only one who occupies it.

Cultivate a Sense of Humor

Because sex is so intense, every couple experiences times of awkwardness in addition to times of satisfying intimacy. All these experiences added together create a legacy of sexual love in your relationship. Your ability to meet one another's needs along with your ability to laugh together at your times of awkwardness will continually add value to your love.

One couple with a fourth grade son were having difficulty finding time to enjoy one another sexually. Their careers were in full swing, their son was a very energetic young man, and they were increasingly becoming involved in their church. Out of desperation one Sunday they came up with what they thought was a great idea. They told their son, "John, we've got a new game for you to play. You know we live in this condominium complex and from the balcony, you can see most of the neighborhood. What would you think about playing detective by standing on the balcony and calling out what people are doing?"

Being a curious boy, John enthusiastically agreed. Mom and dad thought they would be able to steal away to their bedroom and enjoy each other while John was announcing the activity of the neighborhood. As they settled into bed they began to hear their son.

"Two boys are riding by on bicycles. Mr. Kennedy is taking out the trash. I wonder if he has any top secrets in the bag he is throwing away? I see a kid on a skateboard. Four girls are skipping rope."

At this point, the parents thought everything was going very smoothly when John announced, "The Andersons are having sex."

They both bolted up into a sitting position and shouted, "How do you know they are having sex?"

To which John replied, "Their kids are on the balcony, too!"

We hope our kids see your kids on the balcony real soon.

What She Really Means

If she says...	She means
We need…	I want…
It's your decision.	The correct decision should be obvious by now.
Do what you want.	You'll pay for this later.
You're so manly.	You need a shave and you sweat a lot.
This kitchen is so inconvenient.	I want a new house.
I want new curtains.	And carpeting and furniture and wallpaper…
I heard a noise.	I noticed you were almost asleep.
Do you love me?	I'm going to ask for something expensive.
How much do you love me?	I did something today you're really not going to like.
I'll be ready in a minute.	Kick off your shoes and find a good game on TV.
You have to learn to communicate.	Just agree with me.
I'm sorry.	You'll be sorry.
Do you like this recipe?	It's easy to fix, so you'd better get used to it.
All we're going to buy is a soap dish.	It goes without saying that we're stopping at the cosmetics department, the shoe department, I need to look at a few new pocketbooks, those pink sheets would look great in the bedroom, and did you bring your checkbook?
You're certainly attentive tonight.	Is sex all you ever think about?

What He Really Means

If he says...	He means
I'm hungry	I'm hungry.
I'm sleepy.	I'm sleepy.
I'm tired.	I'm tired.
Do you want to go to a movie?	I'd eventually like to have sex with you.
Can I take you out to dinner?	I'd eventually like to have sex with you.
May I have this dance?	I'd eventually like to have sex with you.
What's wrong? (first time)	I don't see why you are making such a big deal out of this.
What's wrong? (second time)	What meaningless self-inflicted psychological trauma are you going through now?
What's wrong? (third time)	I guess sex tonight is out of the question.
I'm bored.	Do you want to have sex?
I love you.	Let's have sex now.
I like the way you cut your hair.	I liked it better before.
Yes, I like the way you cut your hair.	$50.00 and it doesn't look any different!
Let's talk.	I am trying to impress you by showing that I am a deep person and maybe then you'd like to have sex with me.[11]

Waffles and Spaghetti in Conflict

Hot Waffles and Simmering Marinara

❝I married Miss Right. I just didn't know her first name was Always.❞

Differences between genders accompanied by differences in personality guarantee that every couple will experience conflict. You will disagree with one another, you will argue with one another, and you will irritate one another. But conflict doesn't have to be destructive to the relationship. Conflict can, in fact, heighten your understanding of what is really important in your relationship if you know how to make it work for rather than against you.

As in everything we have talked about in this book, we do not want to overstate the case about the differences between men and women, but when it comes to conflict, we certainly do not want to ignore the unique traits we *bring* to the process of getting along. Husbands and wives each make contributions to the ups and downs of their relationship. In general, wives smile and laugh more than their husbands.[1] Men find this intoxicating. A smile makes his wife more attractive to him, and when she laughs, especially at his attempts to be humorous, she gets even prettier in his eyes. This is one of the reasons conflict is inevitable in every relationship. It feels so good to have a smiling, laughing wife that every husband wants it to be that way all the time. Even though he knows it is unrealistic, the desire lingers in his heart.

Both men and women experience periods of dissatisfaction in their relationships. And while they experience distress for similar reasons, as they process the disappointments they respond in different ways. Wives complain and criticize more than their husbands.[2] Because a woman's life is made up of connections, she feels the stress of discord. Her first instinct is to talk through it, and when the atmosphere has turned negative it makes sense to her to express the negative emotions she is feeling. Often her distressed words force the couple to discuss subjects which otherwise would be avoided.

When conflict arises, the husband's first reaction is often fear of failure. His confidence about conflict resolution is usually not as high as his wife's. He has been out-talked by her many times, and he has received "the look" even more often. He doesn't really understand "the look" because he can't do it, but he has noticed that every woman he has ever met can do it. "The look" is a very useful tool for women and can accomplish many objectives. When she is upset with her husband, "the look" will often get him to stop whatever it is he is doing. When she is disappointed in his behavior, "the look" can spur him to action that is more pleasing to her. When her kids are out of line, "the look" can bring them into compliance with the plan quicker than anything dad can do. I have seen men try to use "the look," but on his face it is comical. All I can figure is that it must have been attached to the rib that Adam passed on to Eve. Because men often get outplayed in the conflict game, husbands present more excuses than their wives and withdraw emotionally more often.[3]

Win/Win Propositions

Research has shown that men like to compete. When physical or chaotic situations present themselves men respond with a call to action. They feel the need to win by conquering the challenge. Sports, money challenges, a dare from a friend, or a necessary project all fit the bill. Women also feel the need to compete, but it arises in an entirely different way. When the relationships of her life are out of order she feels the call to action. A wife will use competitive tactics when the conflict involves the development or maintenance of key relationships.[4] It has also been shown that women will experience anger when they are faced with uncontrollable situations such as snowstorms or emotional deadlocks.[5]

Successful couples learn the secret of fighting *for* their relationship rather than *against* one another. Because they both compete, they can complement each other. The wife will become competitive when there is distress in the relationship and it feels like it is getting out of control. If her husband doesn't withdraw from the discussion, he will become competitive in the face of the challenge from his wife. If husbands and wives will encourage these instincts in one another, they can compete together for the health of their love. To be sure, these can be explosive situations that need to be disarmed. There are a number of skills that will diffuse the tension in your relationship, and they all have one thing in common—they each use ordinary words in unexpected ways.

Cut the Hot Lead

Periodically your spouse will say things that upset you. Words such as, "You are so insensitive! Why can't you just get it right? That was stupid. You never listen to me. You always have to have it your way," are common in relationships. You grow dependent on each other and then get disappointed. You have bad days when your attitude goes south. When your spouse ignites the conversation, you have a choice. You can react and shorten the fuse, or you can diffuse the situation. At times, the best way to diffuse a conflict is to turn the focus of the conversation. When your spouse launches a verbal grenade, it usually has a compliment embedded in it.

One day Pam and I were talking about a project we were trying to get done at home and she said to me, "Bill, you are so picky."

To say that I enjoyed that comment would be a bold-faced lie, but instead of getting angry it occurred to me to say, "I wouldn't have married you if I wasn't so picky."

When your spouse says, "You are impossible," start humming the theme to *Mission Impossible.*

Lest you confuse this with sarcasm, remember that the Bible says, "A gentle answer turns away wrath" (Proverbs 15:1).

These attempts to cut the hot lead before the conversation explodes won't work every time, but sometimes it is all the discussion needs to remind you that you are in love.

Sound the Alert

When you find yourself becoming agitated or upset, say so early. Early warnings are much easier to calm down than raging conflicts. There are times when you don't have a clever comeback to what your spouse says, but you know it hurt your feelings. If the conversation doesn't change you can tell it will become an argument. Let your spouse know what is happening and provide the opportunity to stop the hurt. Say something like, "I could get my feelings hurt over this." "If we keep going like this we are going to get in a fight." "I don't know why that bothered me, but I need us to be a little careful." If these statements are received with compassion, the argument will be averted.

Reroute the Current

"Whenever you do that I get so frustrated!" shouted Gene.

"Whenever I do what?" inquired Betsy with surprised indignation in her voice.

"Whenever you go on and on about all those people you help. You care about so many people and their problems. I just can't handle it. I am tired of hearing about all this stuff!"

"Gene, what is going on? I never knew this upset you. I always thought you liked my sensitivity."

"Well, I used to. I mean I do. Oh, I don't know what I mean. It just makes me mad," Gene admitted, knowing that he was off base but not knowing why he was upset. For some reason, he couldn't just give it up.

Gene got his introduction to the intimacy of irritation. You see, Gene had been attracted to Betsy by her sensitivity. She seemed to care so much about him when they were dating and during the early years of their marriage. She seemed to be wrapped up in his life and his needs. He was so flattered by the attention and so impressed by her insight that he became jealous when she cared too much about other people instead of him. He wanted the benefits of her sensitivity for himself rather than sharing them with anyone else. As she became more concerned about the needs of those around her and focused less on him exclusively, he felt a growing agony in his heart.

The challenge for Gene is to learn that the very thing he loves most in Betsy is the very thing that irritates him the most. This is a very common scenario played out by married couples. You married your spouse because being together addressed very significant needs in your life. You felt special, more complete. As a result, you were drawn close enough to take the big step of commitment and become husband and wife. But then something changed. The things you loved about your spouse appeared to change.

The strong convictions your spouse has about doing the right thing made you feel you could trust her. But now they are becoming an irritation when she turns them on you and your behavior. The concern your husband showed for your emotions and your well-being early in your relationship is threatening when you see him showing the same concern to others. The strong masculinity of your groom that makes you feel safe and secure also makes you feel lonely and isolated because he doesn't talk with you the way you wished. Whatever you appreciate most about your spouse will often be the point of highest irritation!

If you listen to these irritations and are willing to look beyond your anger to the qualities in your spouse that are so vital to your own life, you will find you can build your marriage even when you're struggling. Your irritations can be the springboard to new conversations of intimacy with your spouse.

To take advantage of the insight of your irritations, try the following:

1. Make a list of the characteristics you appreciate most about your spouse. Keep this list in a place where you can review it often. Reminding yourself that you love your spouse is one of the best ways we know of to lasso the whirlwind of modern life.

2. When you begin to get angry, ask yourself, "What did he or she say or do that has got me so upset?" Something was done that triggered strong emotions in your soul. These strong emotions can either be seeds of anger or bridges of

intimacy. If you can identify the trigger event, you will be close to turning it to your advantage.

3. Ask yourself, "What positive quality in my spouse's life is this irritation related to?"

4. Repeat to yourself at least seven times, "I love my spouse for..." inserting the positive quality in his or her life that attracted you in the first place.

Listen to Your Passwords

Every couple gets in conversational binds from time to time. We all have sensitive emotional needs which we have trouble managing. All couples have patterns in their relationship that are counterproductive to the growth of their marriage. When a couple gets stuck in these patterns or an emotional need sidetracks a conversation, it can be recaptured by passwords. Passwords are words or phrases the two of you agree on that allow you to get back on track. They can be humorous or nostalgic statements that have special meaning to the both of you. They are statements that remind you this relationship is important and that you are committed to making it work. They are statements that will break the ice of stalemated conversations because you have agreed ahead of time that they will.

Blake and Jeannie learned that one of their greatest obstacles to marital intimacy was the habit Blake had of trying to fix Jeannie. She would share her concerns about various aspects of their life, and Blake would jump in and offer microwaved solutions. When he did this, she felt put down and heard messages from her past that she wasn't good enough. This became destructive to their marriage as she shifted into self-protection mode to fight off the perceived onslaught from Blake. They talked about a password they could use to remind them they really loved each other and wanted to connect.

Their solution is a stroke of genius. They both love the program *Home Improvement* and connect it with laughter and hope. They decided on the following password, "It looks like Tim Taylor has his toolbox out again." Jeannie had Blake's permission to use this anytime she felt he was trying to fix her. If she felt the feelings of low self-esteem or anger coming to the surface, she could lovingly look into Blake's eyes and use their password. This would cause Blake to stop and think about the effect he was having on his wife. Blake also had permission to use this phrase when he sensed he was trying to fix the situation and he saw that Jeannie was feeling run over in the process. Since they both agreed to incorporate the password there has been more laughter in their home, and there has also been a greater degree of understanding between them. They now feel they have a way of interrupting conversations that had historically gone awry. They no longer sit around after an argument wondering what happened.

One couple at a marriage conference said the concept of men being waffles and women being spaghetti transformed their relationship so their passwords became, "Let go of my Eggo (waffle)" and "Ragu!"

A Word of Caution

The danger of passwords is the temptation to manipulate your spouse. If he or she is upset, you might be tempted to use your password to force your spouse to be "more reasonable" and see things your way. You may also be tempted to throw this password up in his or her face to end conversations that are unpleasant but necessary to the health of your marriage. These passwords must be used with compassion and an honest desire to build a healthier relationship.

Recently, I (Bill) found a way to handle a situation that has been irritating to me for years. I am a one-task-at-a-time man who likes to a start a project and finish it before I begin another. As a result, I tend not to entertain too many ideas. I feel the need to pursue most of the ideas I have to see if they have potential. The only way I can realistically do this is to limit the number of ideas I let myself juggle. When I feel myself getting overwhelmed with the responsibility of my life, I take a break from new ideas. This helps me relax and prepare for the next round of responsibility.

Pam, on the other hand, is an idea person. She pumps them out like sunshine. I am constantly amazed at the unceasing flow that comes out of her mouth. I have come to realize that Pam relaxes by coming up with and discussing new ideas. She uses them to relieve stress. It is as if she escapes the heaviness of responsibility by discussing what could be rather than dwelling on what is. This has the effect of energizing her and getting her prepared to ride out the next wave of responsibility.

This pattern in our life was a source of significant irritation. Oftentimes, when we were sitting around relaxing, Pam would begin to share her growing list of inspirational thoughts about how to make the world a better place to live. As I listened to what seemed to be an endless stream of ideas, I found myself getting worn out. I didn't understand it for a while. It seemed strange to me that this would be such an irritation as I genuinely liked trying new experiences. I finally realized that I was getting overwhelmed because I felt I needed to act on every one of her ideas. If they had been my ideas, I would not have shared them until I was ready to create some action. I assumed Pam was operating the same way, but she wasn't! She seems to develop an overload of ideas. Talking about them helps her weed through them to decide which ones should be adopted and which are just good discussion topics.

When I realized this, I asked Pam if this was true. "Do you think I should take every idea you share with me seriously?"

"Well, of course, I do," she responded indignantly.

"No, what I mean is, should I think that I need to act on every idea you bring up or are some of your ideas just for discussion?"

"A lot of ideas I bring up are just for discussion."

"So you don't feel the need to carry out all the things you bring up?"

"Of course not! I could never do all of them."

"Then why do you bring them up?"

"It is the only way I can get them off my mind. When I freely talk about my ideas the ones I need to act on keep coming up. The ones I need to let go of just go away."

That was when the light went on for me. For the first time in 15 years of marriage I realized I didn't have to feel responsible for every idea Pam came up with. When we were newlyweds, it was flattering to me to be able to take her ideas and make them happen. After we had children, it became harder. When we landed in the middle of a complete list of adult responsibilities, it was downright impossible. It was as if a big weight had been taken off my shoulders. I asked Pam, "When you are sharing ideas that I really don't want to act on, can I say, 'Pam, that is a great idea!'?"

You can't imagine my relief when she said, "I think that is a great idea!"

"That is a great idea" has become a password in our relationship that carries a great deal of meaning for us. Whenever one of us uses this phrase it makes us laugh, but it also is a compliment to the creativity and ambition that we both appreciate about each other. I have found a new way to appreciate Pam in an area that used to leave me feeling as though I could never keep up with her demands.

Looking for a way out of the miscommunication whirlwind? Try listening.

"That's a great idea!"

Dismantle the Core

Despite your best efforts, you are at times going to miss the mark with each other. Try as hard as you do, sometimes you miss your spouse's needs completely and botch things up. Your intentions may have been right, but your behavior was ridiculous. Or maybe your actions were right but your intentions were wrong and your spouse picked up on it. You have probably lived the day that you needed your wife to be kind and sensitive, but instead she was distracted and out of touch. Or the day you needed your husband to protect his schedule so you could make an important appointment was taken up by a golf game because he forgot about your need. When your humanity gets put on display in these awkward expressions, the only path to peace in your relationship is forgiveness. All great relationships are made up of two committed forgivers.

In our ministry, we have tried to pattern forgiveness after Christ and his ultimate act of forgiveness on the cross. To give "forgiveness handles" that you can grasp in a practical way, we have come up with six statements that provide a working definition.

1. **I forgive (name the person) for (name the offense).**

It is important to specifically name the offense. Vagueness in dealing with forgiveness only leads to doubts about whether forgiveness has truly been achieved.

The greatest example of forgiveness in the world is the forgiveness Jesus Christ has offered us. He has granted each of us who would trust him freedom from guilt. This is indeed good news! But the good news starts with a very tough reality. "All have sinned and fall short of the glory of God" (Romans 3:23).

Too often we skip this step. Maybe it is because you think your hurt feelings are your problem. Maybe you are upset by what your spouse did, but you think he or she had the right to do whatever brings happiness. Maybe it is because you are afraid to bring up pains from the past. Or maybe it is because you just didn't know how. If you are looking for a clear path of freedom, you need to be specific.

2. I admit that what happened was wrong.

Paul increases the seriousness of forgiveness in Romans 6:23 when he writes, "The wages of sin is death...." Paul understands forgiveness to be a life-and-death issue that begins with the honest confession of something done wrong. In our politically correct world, we often feel uncomfortable saying something was wrong. We may feel like we are being critical or judgmental. But if nothing wrong was done, there is nothing to forgive. And if the goal is forgiveness with the hope of restored intimacy, you aren't being a critic or a judge—you are taking fearless steps of love.

3. I do not expect (<u>name the person</u>) to make up for what he or she has done.

This is a courageous statement of reality. Your spouse cannot make up for the mistakes that have been committed. The hurt of the action will continue to pain you and the memory of the irritation will linger. Nothing, absolutely nothing, can ever undo what was done. Once an offense is committed, it cannot be uncommitted, so you need to let your spouse off the hook. Even if you apologize for what you did, it doesn't make up for it. Even if you make some sort of restitution for what you did, it doesn't make up for it. If your spouse has hurt you, what you can do is forgive and give the opportunity for repentance. You can't make up for mistakes but you can start over.

The real tragedy in not forgiving shows up here. If you persist in waiting until your spouse makes up for the mistake, the pain of the mistake will control your life. Every time you are reminded of the event the pain will shoot through your heart. Every time you try to trust, the pain will trip you up. The person you were once so much in love with will become unattractive in your eyes and consistently irritating in your heart.

4. I will not use the offense to define who my spouse is.

When you define your spouse by the negative impact he or she has had on your life, you make him or her bigger than life. You certainly make him or her bigger than you, because you have given him or her the ability to determine the state of your life.

When it comes to forgiving yourself for the things you have done, this step is vital. When you define yourself by the things you have done wrong you encourage a process of decay. If you think you deserve an unhealthy life, you will live out an unhealthy life. If you think you deserve to be punished, you will live out a self-destructive life. If you think you are a failure, you will avoid the path of success. If, on the other hand, you define yourself as the object of God's grace and an adopted child who is in line for God's favor, you will pursue healthy avenues of growth and development.

5. I will not manipulate my spouse with this offense.

Manipulation is an attempt to emotionally blackmail another person. It is an attempt to protect yourself from the influence another person has had on you. There is something in the human spirit that believes we can control another's influence through manipulation. The tragedy is that every act of manipulation confirms that the one who hurt you still has control of your life. Your very approach to life shows that you are still afraid of what this person might do to you, so you try to get to others before they get to you. You run in an endless circle of self-protection, never enjoying the freedom of truly living.

Jesus does not constantly bring up our past sins to force us to do his will. Rather, he calls us to walk with him as new creatures who have been set free from the past and our mistakes. We are encouraged to live as saints rather than as recovering sinners. This does not mean God ignores the influence of our past. He has committed himself to helping us grow through our past and reach up to a whole new life. We too would be wise to look forward to the life ahead of us rather than constantly try to overcome the past that is behind us.

6. I will not allow what has happened to stop my personal growth.

This is probably the most important. Too often we allow the sinful offenses of others to dictate the course of our life. It is almost as though we think we are punishing the ones who hurt us by refusing to pull our lives together. Or we are emotionally committed to keeping things the way they have historically been in our families. If our ancestors were bitter, then we are bitter. If our ancestors were prone to depression, then we are prone to depression. This applies to everything from alcoholism and anger to lack of confidence.

Forgiveness is a protection for our relationship. Forgiveness gives us the ability to stay in love for a lifetime. It is especially important considering that research indicates women hold grudges more often—which might be the reason studies also indicate men are less likely to say they are sorry.[6] If you each selfishly hold on to your right to be angry, you will keep your anger and bitterness—but lose each other! Forgiveness sets you both free to love.

Don't be surprised by the conflict in your relationship. If you had no needs and your attitude was always unselfish, you could have constant peace between you. But because yours is a relationship between people, you should expect the waffles and spaghetti to compete for room at the table.

The His and Her Guide to Automatic, Drive Through Cash Machines

HIS:

1. Pull up to Automatic, Drive Through Cash Machine
2. Insert card
3. Enter PIN number
4. Take cash, card, and receipt

THIS IS SO TRUE

HER:

1. Pull up to Automatic, Drive Through Cash Machine
2. Check makeup in rearview mirror
3. Shut off engine
4. Put keys in handbag
5. Get out of car because you're too far from machine
6. Hunt for card in handbag
7. Insert card
8. Hunt in handbag for scrap of paper with PIN number written on it
9. Enter PIN number
10. Study instructions for at least two minutes
11. Hit "cancel"
12. Re-enter correct PIN number
13. Check balance
14. Look for deposit envelope

15. Look in handbag for pen
16. Make out deposit slip
17. Sign checks
18. Make deposit
19. Study instructions
20. Make cash withdrawal
21. Get in car
22. Check makeup
23. Look for keys
24. Start car
25. Check makeup
26. Start pulling away
27. STOP
28. Back up to machine
29. Get out of car
30. Take card and receipt
31. Get back in car
32. Put card in wallet
33. Put receipt in checkbook
34. Enter deposits and withdrawals in checkbook
35. Clear area in handbag for wallet and checkbook
36. Check makeup
37. Put car in reverse gear
38. Put car in drive
39. Drive away from machine
40. Travel three miles
41. Release handbrake

Waffles and Spaghetti
Achieving Together
The Recipe for Success

"A successful man is one who makes more money than his wife can spend. A successful woman is one who can find such a man."

People of both genders love to achieve. The interaction between men and women has not been called the "Battle of the Sexes" for nothing. We are all competitive, ambitious, and stubborn to some degree. It is not fair to say that men love to produce while women love to nurture—both genders love to produce, and we all should see ourselves as intelligent, creative people.

Maybe you have heard about the three fishermen who were fishing when they came upon a mermaid. The mermaid offered them one wish each, so the first fisherman said, "Double my

I.Q." The mermaid did it, and to his surprise he started reciting Shakespeare.

Then the second guy said, "Triple my I.Q." and sure enough the mermaid did it, and amazingly he started doing math problems he didn't know existed.

The third fisherman was so impressed he asked the mermaid to quadruple his I.Q. The mermaid said, "Are you sure about this? It will change your whole life!" The man said, "yes," so she turned him into a woman.[1]

Both men and women feel better about themselves when they have mastered a new concept or found an effective avenue for achieving goals. It is one of the great areas of life that men and women share in common. That is why husbands and wives talk about "building a life together." A family is not built just because you give birth to kids. It is built because you pursue financial, social, developmental, and cultural goals together.

In this pursuit, careers must be decided on. Every couple wants to succeed in their choices of careers and find the balance that works best for their particular family. The assumption that is made too often, however, is that men and women work the same. Husbands assume, and often announce, that their wives would be happier if they would just find work they liked. Wives often muse over how their husbands can seemingly leave their home life at home and their work life at work and never mix the two.

Different from the Get-Go

Men and women do not approach achievement in the same manner. The difference begins to emerge during childhood and appears to last a lifetime. Recently, makers of children's computer games have come to the startling conclusion that boys and girls like different types of games—a fact parents have known for years. "Finally, the computer industry has awakened to the fact that girls have lots of money to spend, but they don't want the same games that boys have," said Chris Byrne, editor of *Market Focus: Toys,* a New York-based trade publication.[2]

Software makers have been hesitant to accept this conclusion not because of the facts but because they were "nervous about demand and fearful of stirring gender issues."[3] Nobody, including ourselves, wants to go so far as to say that girls never like the games boys like, or vice versa, but the fact is that boys and girls find satisfaction in different ways. And what is this difference? "Girls like cooperative play instead of competitive play," Byrne said. "They want to involve their creativity into playtime and some games geared for boys don't offer that."[4] Nancy Deyo and Brenda Laurel, founders of Purple Moon, spent five years studying girls' interests before concluding that girls "don't care about winning and losing," she said. "They want a good story plot, and they want to actually love a character, who they want to be as real to them as their best friend."[5] "What girls and boys value as entertainment is different," said Laura Groppe, president and chief executive of Girl Games, based in Austin, Texas. "Boys get into one subject matter, while girls spread their interests across many fronts."[6]

There it is again—men are like waffles, women are like spaghetti.

This is not just a kid issue, however. Boys and girls take these same traits into adulthood, and we see that their work preferences are significantly different. As a couple, you need a practical understanding of these differences so you can help one another choose careers that are most likely to bring success. In addition, your differences have vital implications of how you can best encourage one another as you pursue your dreams. Let's look first at the differences in how men and women approach work.

Men like to take more risks than women. Generally, men are more willing to take risks and gain a greater level of satisfaction from the risk than their female counterparts. This is not to say that women are afraid of risk or are unwilling to take risks in their career pursuits. It is just that men enjoy it more. Just like the video games where boys are incessantly looking for someone or something to defeat, men are looking for challenges they can conquer. "The study, called *The Testosterone Rush: A Study of Senior Marketing Executives,* found that men 'shot more from the hip,' while women carefully considered the alternatives before choosing a course of action. When it comes to decision-making, men were perceived to be faster on the draw…and were more apt to take risks….Men also 'pay too much attention to the competition,' and are more short-term oriented."[7]

Women like consensus more than men. If you consider that life for the average female is a web of interconnected relationships and issues, it makes sense that relationships and decisions would be interconnected. This does not mean that she has to get along with everybody in the office. It simply means that she will consider the broad impact of her decisions, and she will want the decision to benefit as many of the important people in her life as possible. "Women…build more consensus during decision-making…and acted more thoughtfully when choosing their course of action."[8] It is interesting to note that "men work longer hours" than women but they "perceive significantly lower coworker support compared to women…" and "women are substantially more likely than men to report that they can talk to their coworkers and are close to and appreciated by their coworkers."[9]

As much as we like to think that we all face challenges the same and that we all follow the same leadership styles, research does not support this conclusion. Men and women tend to lead differently. Men typically emphasize the achievement of organizational goals as the highest priority of the work environment while women typically emphasize people and relationships. Men are people of the ladder, women are people of the circle. I think the reason we are uncomfortable with statements such as these is we go too far with them. We think that emphasizing one part of leadership must mean that we exclude the rest. Balanced research, however, reveals that "women leaders emphasize both interpersonal relations and task accomplishment more than do men" and that "women tended to adopt a more democratic style than men."[10] In other words, women tend to take a more connected view of the work environment while men tend to focus on single issues.

Men and women learn differently. One of the reasons men and women approach the workplace differently is that they learn differently. We are able to learn the same information, but we process it differently. "Men, for example, tend to think more in terms of principles, while women think more in terms of relationships. Men generally learn on a less personal level, while women tie thoughts to emotions." This is why "on achievement tests, men score higher on math and spatial concepts, while women outscore men in areas of language."[11]

As a pastor, I see this in operation all the time. Men are consistently talking about the principles of the Bible and how to apply them to our lives. Women are more concerned about the well-being of the members of their families and the spiritual motivation of the ones they love. It is also interesting to notice that women have no trouble meeting new women and getting them involved in Bible studies. Men, on the other hand, feel awkward meeting new men and asking them to get involved in anything. The men would rather just make an announcement and expect people to come because of the "principle of the thing."

The fact that women tie knowledge to their emotions is also why women usually have better memories than men. Women attach the events of their lives to their emotions, which makes the memory stronger. When it is time to recover the memory, it is easier to remember because it was more intense for her than for him. Men go through life one activity at a time and usually do not attach it to a vivid emotion. As a result, the memory of the activity is rather bland. In my relationship with Pam, this is a constant frustration. She will often say to me, "Don't you remember?" The problem is, I don't. She has such vivid memories of times we have spent together that at times I wonder if I was really there.

Men and women cope with work stress differently. When men are faced with stress at work, they either focus on the task and get it done, or they divert attention to some other activity that is easier for them. In school, male students will distract themselves by watching more television than their female counterparts. It is almost comical to walk through the student union of any university and watch the young men sitting watching TV while the young women are in huddles talking. Conversely, women seek out conversation with others to cope with the pressures of work. They find that when they can talk through the process of their expectations, they can find handles for facing the stress. A woman will talk with parents, friends, trusted coworkers, or her husband, but the stress remains until she can talk it out.[12]

Women feel they have to work harder than men. Beginning with the high school years, it becomes evident that women definitely feel they have to work harder than men to achieve the same level of success. In high school "women spent more hours in studying and less hours in watching TV. This may be due to the fact that women…tend to attribute their achievement outcomes to effort while men attribute theirs to ability."[13]

Once a woman enters the workforce, she quickly realizes she has entered a male-dominated domain. "Despite a gradual increase in the number of women in managerial roles, they are still estimated to fill only 25% of managerial positions in Germany, 28% in Switzerland, 33% in the UK and 43% in Australia. At higher levels women are even more poorly represented, filling only 10% of senior level management positions in the United States, between 1% and 15% in Australia and 5% in Germany."[14] As a result, women who hope to maximize their careers find they often have to adopt their work style.[15] They would probably prefer to focus on the interrelationships between people and tasks, but they end up having to divide up the work day into single pursuits rather than create a multitasking environment. Researchers Eagly and Johnson discovered in 1990 that women feel the pressure "to adopt more typically male styles in order not to lose authority and position."[16]

The struggle does not stop here, however. Because men are so attached to their work they defend it by making women feel they are not as capable. And, because it is not natural for women to act like men, they are criticized when they try. As a result, women are often placed in "a 'double bind situation.' If they adopt stereotypically masculine styles of leadership that may be required for that particular job, 'they are considered to be abrasive or maladjusted.' However, if women utilize stereotypically feminine styles, they are considered less capable and their performance may not be attributed to competence."[17]

Women are affected more by their home life than men. This is one of the most obvious arenas where the differences between men and women comes into play. Because men see their life in individual boxes, they approach work as if it is its own pursuit. It is not attached to family life, it is not attached to friendships, and it is not attached to the emotional climate of their relationships. When a man goes to work, he goes to work. It has often been said that people need to leave their personal lives at home in order to succeed in their careers. This was obviously first said by a man.

Because women connect everything in life, work is an integrated pursuit. Her day at work affects her relationships at home and her relationships at home affect her work. She would like to separate the two but finds that it is more work to keep them separate than it is to let them relate to one another. As a result, she enjoys her work more when her life at home is going well, and she enjoys her family more when her work is going well.

What Satisfies?

Modern research has brought this important distinction to the surface. "Although women work for less pay and in jobs that are less intrinsically rewarding, they do not appear to be any less satisfied with their jobs than men, a finding that has come to be known as the 'paradox of the contented female worker.'"[18] "These results provide a basis for concluding that job satisfaction is significantly higher among women compared to men when partner support is high. The impact of coworker support on men is much like the effect of partner support on women. That is, job satisfaction among men is maximized by high coworker support, which increases job satisfaction regardless of the level of partner support. Unlike men, the impact of coworker support on women's job satisfaction is conditional because it depends on partner support."[19]

Parenthood impacts men and women differently. When women have children their world expands. Each child gains a place in her heart, and there seems to be no end to the number of children she can love and care for. And because she connects her life together relationally, each new child enhances her life and intensifies her motivation. As a result, she is more motivated to achieve and more satisfied with her career as a mom than prior to motherhood.

Men are not so fortunate. Each child adds a new box to dad's waffle, but kids are not boxes that men can ignore. Whether his children are easy or difficult, each dad must pay attention to his kids. They demand attention and are incessant about having dad involved in their favorite activities. It is an incredible compliment that every kid wants his or her dad involved, but this involvement complicates his life. His career requires significant focus, and he knows that each child should get the same intensity of focus from him. He gets frustrated because he can't keep that many boxes open at once. He must, therefore, open them one at a time, and there are so many in his life when he has a family that it is hard to ever find time to responsibly relax. That is why a dad is less satisfied with his job than a man who has no kids. It isn't that he doesn't like his job, it is just that he is always aware of the stress in his life. He wears down like a battery that is constantly in use.[20] A wise wife will help her husband find time to recharge.

Believe in the Dream

What can a husband do to help his wife be more effective in her career pursuits? He will be a great assistance if he believes in her dream and offers constant encouragement and practical support. She feels her dream intensely, and she cannot ignore the important relationships of her life in order to accomplish that dream. When he becomes involved and makes it possible for her to balance her priorities, she becomes more attached to him and gains confidence in her career.

William Butler Yeats once wrote, "I have spread my dreams under your feet; Tread softly because you tread on my dreams." That's more than just poetry—it's good advice for life. Married life is filled with many transitions. With the transitions often come new plans, new dreams, and new goals. Often these new transitions are met with resistance from the spouse who isn't the dreamer. Change can bring conflict, but it can also bring new possibilities.

Applaud the change. When Bill married me, his dreams and goals were the primary focus of our life. I set aside my schooling to help put Bill through undergraduate then graduate school. We then started a family and eventually God led us to San Diego to pastor a church. That's when my heart changed. Suddenly, my dream to write and speak blossomed. At first Bill resisted my dream. The timing was too inconvenient. We had just begun to build the church, and I had a tiny baby at home. He wanted to be angry, but he soon realized he wasn't fighting me, he was fighting God—and God's calling on my life. Finally, he began to applaud my dream. At first, he tentatively uttered the words, "I believe in you." Then he actually began to believe them himself.

Nourish the change. Bill's first act of applauding the dream was to pay for a one-day writer's seminar sponsored by the San Diego Writer's Guild. In addition, he drove our boys down to the conference so that I could nurse the baby at lunch and again in the afternoon. That was an inconvenience to his schedule, but he wanted to give tangible applause to my dream. The apostle Paul explains this concept in Ephesians 5:28-29, "So husbands ought to love their own wives...for no one ever hated his own flesh, but nourishes and cherishes it..." (NASB). The New International Version renders nourish and cherish as, "to feed and care for." A husband does himself a favor when he loves his wife by building into her personal growth. A wife will want to give back and encourage her husband when she is validated as a growing child of God. Bill believed in me as a writer long before I ever won any awards or published anything of significance. Bill looked at me through God's eyes and responded accordingly.

Clarify the change. You may have valid questions and concerns about your spouse's new plan. As your love compels you to share those concerns, you will have far greater success if you can focus on your concern rather than fault the other. For example, I had several years of schooling ahead when I shared my dream with Bill. We both had a legitimate concern about how to integrate this new responsibility in our schedule and budget. However, Bill didn't attack my character or my dream. Instead he tenaciously set up appointment after appointment until we worked out our differences and found common ground. You'll want to keep talking, week after week, until your feelings catch up to the plan and you "feel" in love again. This is the time to overcommunicate and pray. Many couples have seen that God can change a heart when nagging, yelling, and arguing couldn't.

Cheering to the Finish Line

It's not always easy being teammates. Pam and I had a several-month-long disagreement over her desire to spread her wings. She wanted to return to school and begin work on her writing career. We had a plan and she wanted to jump ahead of schedule. I didn't like it! We still had children who were at home full-time. Pam was a great mom. She was a great wife, lover, and friend. Her desire to chase her goals put pressure on me to help with domestic duties beyond what I thought should be expected of me. Pam's dreams were an inconvenience to my life! And as she looked outside our home for growth I was missing her. My response was to get angry with her! I fought her for months before I came to my senses. I realized I wasn't fighting Pam, I was fighting God. God had placed this dream in Pam and I was blocking it. Pam wasn't trying to make my life miserable—I was choosing that for myself.

I finally came to the point where I could encourage Pam in her pursuits, and I wanted to find a way to make up for the grief I had given her. One day I had to be on campus for a project we were working on at church. Pam would be in class that day, and before she left for school, she said, "Think of me when you are at school today." That's when I got an idea that was as big as the resistance I had been throwing in her way.

She was in a medieval literature class that morning. The professor was leaning against the chalkboard and had just announced that romance was dead. He pointed out that it was an idealistic fallacy in the Middle Ages and unobtainable today. A chorus of women in the room agreed, "Yeah, all men are jerks."

In the middle of this invective on the state of men in our world, I broke into the room unannounced. I walked over to Pam's desk, which was inconveniently located in the middle of the room. I set down a dozen red roses on her desk, bent down over her left shoulder, whispered, "I love you," gave her a kiss, and left the room as quickly as I had come in.

"Is it your birthday?" the startled professor asked Pam.

"No."

"Your anniversary?"

"No."

"Then what's the reason?"

"I guess he just wanted me to know he loves me and he believes in me!"

Then many of the women in the class asked, "Does he have a brother?"

I had fought Pam in a big way as she tried to pursue her dream. I wanted her to know in just as big a way that I believed in her dream.

Anticipate future changes. The birth of a child, job transitions, teen children, midlife emotional adjustments, and the empty nest are just a few changes that the average couple will experience. If you anticipate change, and even embrace it as it comes knocking on your door, you will find change to be a catalyst for growth in your marriage. It's like marrying a new spouse every few years—only this one keeps his or her same name. Just like each night brings a new dream, so each change brings the potential for a new dream that can bring vitality and maturity to your love relationship.

What can a woman do to help her husband be effective in his career pursuits? Keep it simple! When your husband feels he has the freedom to focus on work he gains confidence about his ability to succeed. When your husband senses that his work is part of the family's schedule rather than an interruption to it, his desire to help shape the kids' character will grow. When you say you are proud of him for the work he does, he leaves for work the next morning with renewed motivation. It sounds silly, but the key to helping your husband is to give him your permission to succeed on his career path.

When Pam and I moved to the San Diego area so I could begin my career as a senior pastor, I was very excited. I was convinced God had called me to preach and to minister to families. It was evident that he had led us to a suburb north of downtown, and it was only seven miles from the beach. I hit the pavement running, convinced that this church would grow into a win-win situation for the congregation and my family. It required a pretty intense focus on my part to learn the current processes of this church and diagnose the changes that needed to be made. I assumed that Pam was right behind me in step with the vision.

She was just as committed as I was to the success of our new pursuit, but she was facing different pressures. She was the primary caretaker of our two preschool boys, and we were living in a two-bedroom apartment with a very awkward rule. The rule was that children were not allowed to play on the sidewalk, on the grass, or in the common areas of the apartment complex. The only place kids were allowed to play was in the playground, which was on the other side of the complex.

Now, Pam is usually a very positive individual, but the stress of dealing with two toddlers in a "no playing zone" was more than she could handle. A depression blindsided her and changed her normally supportive position. Instead of being proud of me, I heard things like, "Why did you do this to me?" "How long do we have to live like this?" "Are you ever going to do anything to get us out of this hole?" Coming home after a long day of work was like volunteering for an interrogation. I knew I needed to go home and invest in my family, but I wanted to just spend more time at work. Things were working there and everybody seemed to appreciate my efforts. Pam didn't like the fact that it was easier for me to be at work than with her, but she agreed that it was a critical time in our life.

I (Pam) had given up a nice house, great friends, and a satisfying leadership role for sanctified insanity! Over the next few weeks, a depression hit me like a tidal wave. I was struggling with who I was, what my new role would be in this church and community, and how I would survive such a drastic change.

One day I went to the closet to get something off the top shelf. In reaching for the box, everything off the top shelf fell on me and scattered across the floor. "I hate it here!" I cried. The next thing I knew, I was sitting on top of a load of laundry and I was sobbing! I don't know how long I sat there but in toddled my two little boys.

"Mommy, what's wrong?" they asked.

I moaned, "I don't know."

I gathered them onto my lap and rocked them as I prayed, "God, I know this is not the abundant life you planned! Bill has been paying a huge price. He's been coming home to complaints and my whining. I have been believing lies about him. I've said some awful things, like, 'You don't care about me!' (and I know he does) and, 'Your job is more important than me and the kids.'" (That is definitely not true!) I looked around my pathetic setting and cried out to God, "Help me figure out what to do!"

I sat and rocked my boys to sleep then picked them up and put them to bed. I pulled out my Bible and read a very familiar passage in Ephesians 5. One phrase seemed to be in neon lights! "...the wife must respect her husband." I looked at it again. *Are you sure about this, God? Isn't there a loophole for situations like mine?* Over the next few days, I read the dictionary and the thesaurus looking up synonyms of honor and respect. I came up with three things I needed to do.

1. *See Bill as God sees Bill*—a man worthy of respect because God created him.

2. *Talk to Bill the way God talks to Bill*—with loving, encouraging but honest words.

3. *Treat Bill like God treats Bill*—by building him up with kindness.

A few days later, I called Bill up and asked to take him to lunch. He responded rather tentatively with, "I think so." He wasn't too sure what he was going to get from me.

Over lunch, I reached across the table, took his hand, and said, "I'm sorry for the way I have treated you. I just want you to know, if I never get the things I think will make me happy, that's okay. From this day forward I am on your team!"

I (Bill) can hardly explain the impact those words had on me. I have learned that the most important opinion in life to me is Pam's. When she says I am doing well, I truly believe I am doing well regardless of what others might say. On the other hand, when she is disappointed or critical, my heart sinks. I want to immediately change her opinion, and if I run into a roadblock in doing that I instinctively want to shut her out of my career decisions. So when she said, "I am on your team," my perspective on life was transformed. In just a few days after that lunch it became clear to me how to move my family into a rental home with a yard that took the pressure off. I also began to see how to spend more strategic time with the family that made Pam feel she was not alone in caring for our children. All of this added together to simplify my relationship with her, which freed me up to concentrate on my work more effectively. The key was that Pam made my life simpler with her commitment to be on my team and that made all the difference.

Deliberate Dreams

What can you do as a couple to make your pursuits more effective? Be deliberate. The differences in the sexes will lead to some predictable outcomes if you do not deliberately set goals and organize responsibilities. If left unchecked, the husband becomes more and more focused on his career and spends increasing numbers of hours in the pursuit of financial success. Meanwhile, more and more of the responsibilities of the home become hers to manage. The end result is that she feels taken advantage of and he feels unappreciated. Nobody grows closer to people that take advantage of them and make them feel unappreciated. A couple without goals will either live a very simple existence so this cycle never starts, or they will see the slow and steady deterioration of their love. Couples with goals they agree on will find their achievements make them more interesting people who consistently have new material to talk about.

So what types of goals does a couple need to actively set in order to maximize achievement without eliminating intimacy? In order to maintain a balanced life, it is helpful to write goals in four major life areas. Write goals that will help you take another "STEP" forward. You'll want to develop:

Your Spiritual Life

Your Team

Your Energy

Your Productivity

Your spiritual life. This area includes goals that build a closer walk with God. For example, a daily personal devotional time with God, Bible studies, church attendance, verses you'd like to memorize, and growth activities such as retreats, conferences, Christian radio, and books you'd like to read. When you are connected to God, your perspective is renewed, and your decision-making skills sharpen because you will be thinking more like him.

Your team. Included in this section are goals that will build into your significant relationships, like marriage, family, and close personal friends. One author recommends that we prioritize our lives by who will cry at our funeral.[21] When you maintain healthy relationships, then you will have more emotional stability to tackle life. Your motivation for life will increase as your relationships are strengthened. This is where you would divide home responsibilities so that the stuff of everyday life does not rob your desire for one another.

Your energy. To maintain a high level of energy you must manage the areas of life that are of importance to you as an individual. This will include your personal finances, emotional well-being, health, and social life. It will also include those activities that are vital to you as an individual: hobbies, sports, reading, leisure activities, and areas of study or crafts.

Your productivity. This area includes goals in your career, education, and ministry (both public and personal). What type of work do you want to pursue? What position do you want to attain to in that field? What type of education do you need to fulfill these pursuits? Who are the people you would like to personally influence for Christ? How would you like to use your gifts in your local church ministry?

How to Write a Goal

To know whether you are making any headway on a dream, you need to write a set of goals that explain how to get to the dream.

A goal must be specific. How will you know you've fulfilled a dream unless you can articulate what that dream looks like? For example: A nonspecific goal would be: "I'd like to be happy." Well, what makes you happy? What are you like when you are happy? Is happy something that God even wants you to set as a goal?

A better example might be: "I'd like our family to have an income that would adequately supply our housing, food, and basic lifestyle desires." You could then list those desires and estimated costs to come up with a target income need.

After that you could brainstorm on how to meet that income need and decide if meeting the need is worth the required lifestyle. If meeting the income is too great a strain, you might adapt the list, look for another geographic location, or look at other income-creating options.

Goals must be realistic. I cannot write a goal that I cannot control. For example, I can't say, "I wish I were Afro-American or Hispanic." That is out of my control. I also can't say, "I wish my husband were more romantic." You can't control your husband. You can, however, be more romantic yourself, provide opportunities for relaxed romance, and openly communicate your romantic desires and feelings. But you can't *make* him be romantic.

Goals need to be achievable with God's help. We want goals that are just out of our power to achieve because these kind of goals stretch us and make our faith grow. Each speaking engagement that comes in for Bill and me is a faith builder. We can let people know we are available, but we really believe God fills our speaking slate. We can't make anyone invite us in.

In business, all you can do is be persistent at working your plan, then trust that God will work behind the scenes to make the connections you can't. In matters with your children, your goal is to be an excellent, compassionate parent, but all parents realize that a child can't be with you 24 hours a day, especially as they grow up, but God can be with them.

But I Hate Goals!

Sometimes people feel overwhelmed by the goal-setting process. Goal-setting may feel the same as being asked to paint the Empire State building with a toothbrush. It doesn't have to be that overwhelming. Think of goal-setting the same as climbing stairs. You want to get to the top and each stair (goal) helps you get there.

Other times people feel like they can't obey God and at the same time set goals. Somehow they feel they are usurping his control or direction. That is impossible!! We are not in control of our futures. There are always variables we cannot control. But we are stewards of our futures, and we are commanded to "be very careful, then, how you live—not as unwise but as wise, making the most of every opportunity, because the days are evil" (Ephesians 5:15-16).

The key is flexibility, that is, ranking our will under God's will. We set goals with the attitude of, "This is our educated guess at life. God, if you want it changed, we know you'll make it very clear!" The commands of God found in the Bible are an expression of his goals for us. Often he leaves the application of the goals up to us.

Sometimes couples experience one spouse liking and desiring goals while the other drags his or her feet. That can be manageable with a good attitude. Bill likes the concept of goal-setting, but early on I discovered he didn't like the process of writing out his or our goals. So I interviewed him. Each year, usually as we travel on family vacation, Bill and I talk about our plans and review where we are and where we're going. I play vice president and record the conversation in the form of written goals. Then, because I'm not fond of spreadsheets, Bill writes financial objectives that need to be accomplished to fund our dreams. After this process, we sit down and reevaluate our goals, make scheduling adjustments, discard some, or place some in a "not now, but in the future" file. We try to be teammates using each of our strengths to benefit our team.

"Why It's Great to Be Male" facts...

1. We know stuff about tanks.

2. A five-day trip requires only one suitcase.

3. We can open all our own jars.

4. We can go to the bathroom without a support group.

5. We can leave a motel bed unmade.

6. We can kill our own food.

7. We get extra credit for the slightest act of thoughtfulness.

8. If someone forgets to invite us to something they can still be our friend.

9. Everything on our faces stays the original color.

10. Three pairs of shoes are more than enough...maybe too many.

11. Car mechanics tell us the truth.

12. We can sit quietly and watch a game with a friend for hours without thinking, "He must be mad at me."

13. Same work—more pay.

14. Gray hair and wrinkles only add character.

15. We can drop by and see a friend without having to bring a little gift.

16. If another guy shows up at a party in the same outfit, we just might become lifelong friends.

17. Our pals will never trap us with: "So, notice anything different?"

18. We are not expected to know the names of more than five colors.

19. We are totally unable to see wrinkles in our clothes.

20. The same hairstyle lasts for years—even decades.

21. We don't have to shave below the neck.

22. A few belches are expected and tolerated.

23. Our belly usually hides our big hips.

24. We can do our nails with a pocketknife.

25. Christmas shopping can be accomplished for 25 people on the day before Christmas and in 45 minutes.[22]

Waffles and Spaghetti at Home

Who Does What When and Why

"A woman marries a man expecting he will change, but he doesn't. A man marries a woman expecting that she won't change and she does."

A beleaguered young mom went to an "Organizing Your Life" class. After hearing many organizing tips, she asked, "But how do you get your kids to help clean up? I have two young children, and it's usually easier to just clean up myself. That way, I know where things are, and they get put away right. But I feel frustrated about that."

Another woman in the class answered, "In our house, we use a 'Butler Box.' Whenever something is left lying around the house where it doesn't belong—even if it's car keys or a wallet— it gets put into a large, wooden box that we call the Butler Box.

Then, if anyone is looking for something that's lost and finds it in the Butler Box, he can't just grab it out. He has to do five minutes of chores around the home to get the object back."

"What a clever idea!" the first woman said. "How old were your children when you started that?"

"Children?" the second woman answered. "We don't have any children. This is for my husband."[1]

Despite the frustration between men and women, it remains an undeniable fact that men and women still desire to live together. People long for the stability of companionship, the security of emotional acceptance, and the passion of sexual desire. When a man and woman become a couple, they enter into marriage with the expectation that joy and happiness will follow. Then life gets in the way of living. Bills need to be paid, chores endlessly demand our attention, cars need to be maintained, and finances must be managed.

So how does a couple go about dividing up the responsibilities of life? What chores does the husband oversee? What tasks should the wife be in charge of? What responsibilities should be handled together? Are there chores that are best handled by women? by men? These are questions that have plagued couples throughout history as each generation wrestles with answers that fit the culture of the day.

The challenge of modern couples in the 21st century has been expanded because of the balance between men and women in the workforce. "Since the 1950s, with the exponential increase of women in paid jobs and careers, researchers have discovered much more disagreement between partners regarding housework (approximately 75% of U.S. women now work in paid jobs). Couples now often report that housework constitutes a salient issue in marital strife."[2]

Historically, women's work has centered around the home. It has been assumed that women are more domestic and have a natural desire to develop a nurturing environment in their homes. Men, on the other hand, have been relegated to the areas of yard work, analytical pursuits, and maintenance of the family machinery. It has been assumed that they handle these areas best because they can conquer them.

It is unfortunate that these stereotypes have been established and passed on for generations. We all know men who are good at housework and women who are good with mechanical equipment. An interesting study of 731 urban couples and 178 farm couples has recently revealed that it is not sexuality but availability that enhances one's ability to take care of the home. The researchers "found that partners help each other to the degree they are available and according to the resources they bring to the family...."[3]

We should not overreact, however, and assume men and women will approach the issues of the home in the same manner. Because women have the ability to connect everything in life, the average women can manage several tasks at a time better than the average man. Finding a balance in the operation of the home is a nonnegotiable necessity for her. The tasks she considers vital must be addressed with a workable plan or everything in the home will feel out of place. It doesn't necessarily matter to her if she attends to these tasks or if others in the family get them done as long as they are accomplished. It does not appear that the actual tasks are as important a factor as the balance between all the important chores.

One at a Time

Because men tend to process life in individual boxes, the average man prefers tasks that can be done one at a time. He wants to do the first task until it is done and then move on to the next one. If it is a creative task, he even wants to stay in the box and admire the work for just a little while. Because he loves his wife and feels great about himself when she is proud of him, he usually wants her to join him in admiring the expert craftsmanship of his latest venture. The nature of the task is not as important as the ability to focus on one task at a time.

The key to dividing responsibilities in the home, then, is in assessing the particular system of your relationship. As you evaluate the chores that must be done in your family to keep your life in the order you want, you will discover that some of the tasks are best accomplished in unison with other tasks and will be most strategically handled by the wife. For instance, in our home the family schedule is a task that requires a significant amount of multitasking to keep everyone on track. All three of our boys are active in multiple activities. These include school, sports, music, church involvement, and campus clubs. In addition, Pam and I both have active careers. Coordinating these five aggressive schedules is overwhelming to me, to say the least. I have trouble keeping *my* schedule together let alone the schedules of the rest of the family. We figured out early that we would have to delegate this responsibility to Pam or we would all have to seriously simplify our lives. If it were up to me, there would be a limit of no more than two commitments by each member of the family, and even then I would probably get lost in the process.

Pam, on the other hand, seems to think it is fun to keep all of us moving in productive directions. To me, there is no limit to her ability to envision further success for each of us. The boys and I frustrate her on this point quite often. She effortlessly carries lists in her head and coordinates a large number of commitments with ease while each of us slows down the process with our single-mindedness. We don't intentionally disappoint her—we just can't keep up. We try to make written lists that match the lists in her mind, but even then we pull up short.

We were preparing to leave town for a weekend conference, and I chivalrously volunteered to help with the errands that were necessary. It was obvious this was a welcome offer because Pam immediately rattled off a list of items to be procured. One of these involved picking up laundry at the dry cleaners. As is too often the case, I managed to succeed in every errand except one—and the one I missed this time was the laundry.

You would think I would learn my lesson and write down the list every time, but Pam makes it seem so simple as she talks through it. I set out this day to get all the errands done, but I pulled up short. As soon as I walked in the door, I knew I had blown it. How did she know to ask about the laundry first? It was only one of the errands I had run for her that afternoon, but somehow she knew that inquiring about the dry cleaning would instantly put her in the power position. As the reality of the scene sunk in, my heart sunk into my toes. Pam had her heart set on wearing those clothes this particular weekend. It was too late…the dry cleaner's was closed for the evening, and we had a six o'clock flight the next morning.

Pam had a choice. If she wanted, she could have buried me with the evidence of my poor performance. She could have justifiably said, "I just can't trust you with these types of things." She could have laid on the guilt with statements such as, "I am so disappointed. I had my heart set on wearing those clothes. You know I don't look as good in the other outfits I will now have to wear." Instead, she swallowed her disappointment and chose to be grateful. She told me later that she struggled to conclude, *He's a great guy. He didn't mean to forget my clothes. If this is the worst I have to put up with, I guess I've got it pretty good.* If only I was better at writing things down, Pam wouldn't have to be so good at forgiving.

But this is not even the clearest example of why Pam needs to be in charge of the coordination of all our schedules. Our oldest son was in a community drama when he was nine years old. He had evening rehearsals, and one of those evenings Pam asked me to pick him up when I was done with work because only one car was working that day. I thought it was a good plan so I heartily agreed—but I didn't write it down. I had an appointment that evening and then went to the hospital to visit an individual in our church. When I left the hospital I breathed that sigh of relief that comes at the end of an effective workday and headed home. It felt good to be done for the day, and I was looking forward to going home to spend a little time relaxing. I walked in the door and had a contented look on my face until Pam asked, "Where is Brock?"

Don't you hate that sinking feeling that hits you in the stomach and then drains the blood all the way out your toes? The reality of what I had not done hit me like a ton of bricks. I couldn't believe I had forgotten my son. Fortunately, one of our close friends was the director of the production, so Brock had gone home with her. I quickly left to pick up my very sleepy youngster and brought him home to his relieved and frustrated mother. I have since come to embrace the wisdom of the statement: *the faintest of ink is better than the best of memory.*

Work the System

As you look at your family system, you will discover that many tasks in your home are best done in conjunction with others. These will most likely be preferred by the wife. Some of the tasks, however, are best accomplished as individual tasks and will typically be better handled by the husband. In our home, I oversee all the car maintenance, which is a predictably male activity, but it surprises some to learn that I usually do the laundry also. As Pam and I analyzed the way we work as a couple, we recognized that Pam's creativity can get in the way of mundane tasks like laundry. She will get the laundry sorted and put the first load in, but then her creative juices start to flow and she becomes involved in other tasks. Once she is in high gear it is quite possible she will not get back to the laundry to finish it. I prefer to focus on one task at a time, so when I am doing the laundry, I am doing the laundry. I may "fiddle" around with some other activities, but they are only diversions to keep me busy while I am waiting for the next step in the main task of getting our clothes clean.

What It Takes

To get on the same page of life, you'll want to find out what is really important to each of you. Often arguments and misunderstandings develop because we assume we know what is important to one another. But priorities are deceptive. They shift around like the pea in the shell game. You don't want to be guessing when you dovetail your life together, you want to *know* what is important!

For a really long time, I assumed Bill's work around the house and yard was out of necessity. I thought he felt he had to mow the grass and fix the car and do home improvements because we couldn't afford to hire them out. When things got busy and the "Honey Do" list grew, I felt bad because Bill's precious few days off had to be spent around the house. Then we had "the talk."

Bill was working on finishing a project on our unfinished home. The younger boys needed closet doors hung in their room. Bill worked painstakingly hard all day to finish the job before out-of-town company arrived. When he came down and announced they were done, I ran upstairs and looked, gave him a hug and said thanks, and off I went. After about half an hour of getting things ready for our guests, I began looking for Bill. I knew he was done with the closets, but I couldn't find him. I checked the shower (a logical place to go after a dirty job and ten minutes before guests arrive). I looked in the garage, the office, outside in the yard, then I finally charged up the stairs. Bill was still standing in the exact place I'd left him 30 minutes before. He was gazing at his closet door creation!

"You're still here! Bill, they look terrific. What's wrong?"

"Nothing. It just feels so good to be done with something!" Bill exclaimed. "All day long every day, I work with people. People are never done—at least, not this side of heaven. Those doors are done! They're done!"

Now, I understood why Bill took so long to do each project. He wanted the project to be done well—and stay done! The list of chores that I thought were a cumbersome drag Bill sees as a gold mine. Those chores bring balance to his life. Bill is talented with landscaping and woodworking. He built the home we live in. What drives him crazy is that it isn't done! Now I know that he desires a portion of his time to be spent on what he calls "mindless work with his hands."

We've provided a little quiz for each of you. Write each of the following "Life Responsibilities" on 3x5 cards. You will each need a set. Rank each item with a 1, 2, or 3. A 1 means it is very important to you. You would keep your 1 activities even if you never could do a 2 or 3. A 2 means it is important, though not a main focus, but you don't feel like it can go undone. A 3 means if it gets done fine, but if it doesn't, no sweat. The 3s are those things that can drop out of life when things get hectic or the quality can suffer a bit and it doesn't make you crazy.

Life Responsibilities

___Being in good physical shape

___Having a neat, clean home

___Having your family finances in order

___Maintaining correspondence

___Having quality intimacy/romance
___Having time with your children (like overseeing home-
   work, team parent, etc.)
___Having fun as a family (like trips, vacations, kick around
   time)
___Succeeding in your career
___Having a personal ministry/involvement in church
___Extracurricular activities (like community involvement,
   career enhancement, philanthropic activities)
___Having a nice car(s)
___Furthering your education
___Achieving more financial success
___Time alone
___Time with God
___Time with mate (talking, relating nonsexually)
___Time for a hobby
___Other_____

Now compare your cards. Which things are ranked the same?
Mark those with a *. You're probably less likely to argue over
those areas. Circle the areas that have the greatest differences
(when yours is a 1 and his is a 3!). You'll have to negotiate in
those areas. They are hot spots.

Now prioritize the cards. Maybe a neat house was marked in
the survey above. But one of you marked the kitchen and dishes
as a 1 and the other marked the bathrooms. Clean means different things to different people. Bill and I found out early in
our marriage that the bedroom and the living room need to be
neat for me to be happy. Bill has to have a clean kitchen with the
dishes done and put away or he can't relax. We should take
responsibility for that which is a high priority to us! I make the
house overall orderly and organized (that is, on the surface my
house looks good!). As our life has picked up its pace, Bill has

taken on the responsibility for the dishes. Either he does them, or he delegates them to the boys. He deep cleans the kitchen regularly.

I am responsible for all our family heirlooms and emotional caretaking (photo albums, baby books, Christmas cards, and letters to friends). Bill is responsible for de-junking our closets and lives regularly. I am too sentimental. Everything reminds me of a story or a memory, so it's *much* too valuable to part with. However, I rarely miss what is tossed! The only rule Bill has is that he makes a "debatable bin" that I review before he empties it.

Another area of possible conflict will be those areas you both marked as 3s but in reality are 1s in daily life. For example, neither Bill or I love to fiddle with finances, but whether we like it or not, bills have to be paid! Because Bill was a math major and he's great at it, he's taken it on. But I have pity on him and his sacrifice, so I will usually bake him chocolate chip cookies and then sit down to sort out the bills or write out the checks or file—something to keep him company.

Sold to the Highest Bidder

When I was a little girl, I played a parlor game called "Pit." It was a mock version of the trading that happens on Wall Street. Daily, brokers trade commodities on the stock exchange. In the game "Pit," players would try to gather all of one commodity, say, corn. They would trade other players for the commodity they prized most. One player might trade four wheat just to get two corns. That is exactly what you'll need to do when you come to the negotiating table with your spouse. If something is really important to you, you'll have to compensate in other areas. The priority is to arrive at one dovetailed life.

"I'll trade you childcare on Mondays and Thursdays if you'll do this stack of errands. I hate errands!" Bill exclaimed.

"That's fair. I need the time for ministry appointments, business, and writing errands, so those errands will fit in between. And since I'll be running back and forth, I'll pick up the boys from school. That way you can have some uninterrupted time to work on the house and yard and do paperwork and bills."

"That's workable. Who's going to take this stack of responsibilities?" he asked as he picked up the level 3 cards that neither of us wanted but knew had to get done.

"Let's see. What's in it?"

"Laundry. Let's divide and conquer on that. If you sort it all on Monday, I'll wash and fold it the next few days, then Thursday you can oversee the boys as they put it away. Fair?"

"Fair. How about lunches?"

"The boys can make their own. They can each take responsibility for keeping a car clean this year too."

"Good idea. I'll take homework and any errands that come with that," I volunteered.

"Great. But I'll still set aside one day close to science fair time to help," said Bill.

"Of course. That's tradition now. How about this stack of ministry priorities?"

"Let's take that on our getaway and pray over those. We need to decide which to do now, which to have our new staff person do, and which are great ideas for the future. Pam, you can easily fill your days with good things and not get to your writing. God has called you to that, so we have to help you get some boundaries on your life so you can do it."

I looked at my pile of 1s. Romance for Bill and me, the boys' activities and daily homework and bedtimes, writing, women's ministry, exercise. It would be tough to get all the 1s accomplished if I didn't set up some boundaries on my life and protect that time. I remembered the year Bill fought to get my attention. He missed me and wanted more time with me. That's how the cards all started. Bill and I both wanted more time together, and we were having a tough time finding it. I smiled.

"What are you smiling about?" Bill asked.

"I'm just remembering how this got started."

"Desperation."

"Yeah, but it's paying off. Every year, it's easier to negotiate responsibilities. There are less arguments between times and best of all, I really do have more time with you."

"Hey! Who's going to take the windows?"

We both pointed to each other. Shook our heads no.

"Back to the bargaining table."

Don't Talk About It, Be About It!

There are only 24 hours in a day, and as a team you have to come up with a workable plan on how to spend those hours. In most families, resources are also limited, so you'll need one plan on how to spend or save your funds.

For several years, Bill started noticing that his exercise time was getting shorter and shorter, and he was getting rounder and more out of breath. This year his exercise priority went from a 2 to a 1 with stars and exclamation points around it! Bill decided he was willing to trim his schedule in a few areas to make working out a priority. For me, writing and speaking are not only my career, they are what I truly enjoy, so they are a high priority. But equally as high is time spent caring for my children. I love helping with science projects, going to the library, reading aloud to them, so I gave up other things so I can do that. I spend less time socializing with friends, I rarely shop for fun, and if I have to choose between cleaning the house or reading to the boys, I choose the reading.

As a couple, it is vital that you deliberately divide up labor between the two of you because, although men and women remain different from one another, the culture we live in has been swiftly changing over the last half century. It used to be that the husband was the main provider for the family and the wife was the primary caretaker. John would conquer the world to bring home the bacon while Jane cooked the bacon, cleaned the house, and nurtured the children. In that culture, it was relatively easy to designate household responsibilities because peoples' options were simple and few.

Consider, however, the world we currently live in. More women are participating in the workforce than any other generation. As women are exercising their opportunity to build careers, men are being more conscientious about their influence with their children. "With regard to dual-earner families, men's greater involvement [today vs. previously] in relationships, caring, and parenting likely is the hallmark of the 1990s."[4]

When you look at everything it takes to smoothly operate a household, you will pretty quickly conclude that household labor appears to be divided equally. People in Detroit were asked to answer the following questions:

1. Who repairs things around the house?

2. Who mows the lawn?

3. Who shovels the sidewalk?

4. Who keeps track of money/bills?

5. Who does grocery shopping?

6. Who gets the husband's breakfast on workdays?

7. Who straightens up the living room when company calls?

8. Who does the evening dishes?

"Not surprisingly, given this measurement procedure, by emphasizing three masculine and three feminine tasks (with two 'neutral') the authors found a relatively equal division of labor."[5]

But we must be careful here. When you count up the number of tasks each partner anchors for the sake of the family, the number may be very close. When you count up the amount of time involved, however, you may come up with a very different picture. "The reason is that feminine tasks require more time. For example, Manke et al. (1994) found that their sample of families spent an average of 2 hours and 40 minutes doing feminine tasks, 51 minutes performing masculine tasks, and 1 hour and 29 minutes doing gender neutral tasks per day. These figures indicate that feminine tasks occupy 53%, masculine tasks occupy 17%, and neutral tasks take 30% of the housework day.

"Other research indicates a similar pattern: Women's work takes more time than men's."[6]

If a couple is not deliberate in defining who will do what and relies simply on traditional roles, they will probably find themselves out of balance. Either the wife will end up working more total hours than her husband and resent him for it, or they will both live in consistent conflict as they are surrounded by unfinished tasks.

Modern research reveals some evidence for a very interesting trend among men and women. Because men are problem solvers by nature, they will tend to want to divide labor so it is fair. A typical husband will want an equitable arrangement (however he defines "equitable").

Women, on the other hand, because they are driven to connect all of life together, will want help with the mundane tasks they are responsible for. The typical wife will interpret it as love when her husband gets involved with daily household chores. She will think he cares and appreciates what she does because he values it enough to get involved. You would think that she would also include his responsibilities in the discussion and that she would want to get involved in the things he must get done. But this does not seem to be the case.[7]

There is, in our modern world, a desire to say that we can design our lives any way we want. We have seen in the last three decades an attempt to make everything generic when it comes to gender differences. The tone of the conversation has been that women are the underprivileged class who have been oppressed by men. The goal has been to rewrite the script so that men and women have equal opportunity and equal choice in the pursuits of their lives.

Despite these efforts and the advantages brought about by technology, there are many aspects of our relationships that have just not changed. In *Men and Women: How Different Are They?*, John Nicholson addresses this interesting development:

> We cannot leave the subject of motivation without commenting on the fact that while a man can pursue professional success with single-minded determination, a woman usually has to divide her time and energy between her job and a second career, that of housewife and mother.

> Getting married has a very different effect on the career prospects of a couple who take the plunge together: it reduces the time a wife can devote to her career, while it may actually increase the working hours available to her husband. Surprising though it may seem, sociologists find that technological progress has had no discernible effect on the time a housewife spends on housework. The average American housewife today spends the same number of hours—fifty-three a week—on domestic chores as her grandmother did, and there is no reason to think that the position is different in other countries. Moreover, despite the demand that men should share the burden, there is little evidence that this is happening.

Even when they have no children, working wives still tend to do the bulk of the shopping, washing and cleaning. When there are children, it is found that a husband's contribution to the running of the house actually declines with each child, while the housework done by his wife increases by 5 to 10 percent for each child. These statements are based on the observations of a team of social scientists working in twelve different countries, in Eastern and Western Europe and in North and South America, and they found surprisingly little variation between one part of the world and another.[8]

Why is this? It has been conclusively shown that men are no more career-oriented than women, and men and women are both primarily motivated by love for their families. "Specifically, research does not support the assumption that men (vs. women) are more career-centered: Instead, and similar to women, men are typically more concerned with their families than their careers; research indicates that about twice as many men are invested in their families as opposed to their careers."[9] So it can't be that men have simply refused to be better at home.

We believe that what we are seeing is the result of stress choices being made by couples. With each year that passes in the life of a couple, responsibility gets larger. With each child that is born, the stress level of the family increases along with the joy of a new life. As the total amount of responsibility grows, choices must be made about how time and talent will be allocated. It seems that women are drawn to the activities of the family because it creates connections with each member of the family. As connections are formed, life becomes more satisfying for her.

Men, on the other hand, drift toward the tasks of the family that require simplified focus. On average, men spend more time at work than women because they can stay focused on one area of life rather than all the areas that are active at home with the family.[10] Dad typically does the yard work because he can focus on the one task at hand while he takes a break from the changing needs of the family.

There is no universal list of women's work and men's work, but there is a tendency for women to gravitate toward those activities that create connections while men collect tasks that require one focus at a time. Early on in the relationship, these differences may not be evident but as the stress level grows in the family these differences become more prominent. Rather than try to change one another, the wise couple will utilize the differences to maximize the effectiveness of the family. The only thing that will hold you back from an effective plan is your attitude. So remember, the important issue is not who does what task, it's the attitude you do it with.

Waffles and Spaghetti As Parents

Belgian Basics and Pasta Principles

"A house is made of walls and beams; a home is built with love and dreams."

When our boys were little they had a habit of getting hurt. If both Bill and I were standing close by our reactions were similar—yet different. While we'd both run to the aid of our son, many different thoughts would be going through our heads. Mine might sound like:

I have to see if he is okay. Looks like it. No broken bones, he's breathing, a little blood, scraped knee. "Okay, buddy, you'll be all right." I need to help him balance this. It's okay to express emotion, but I don't want him to be a wimp. If he's a wimp, then he'll be made fun of at school, his self-esteem will take a hit, and then he will make poor choices, maybe get into drugs, or drinking. But then again, if I don't allow him to express emotion, and he becomes a tough nonemotional male, he'll miss out on the depth of relationships. His kids and wife will feel emotionally distant from him. He could end up divorced or disillusioned and depressed. Oh, my—he could be suicidal! I want more for him than that. I've got to help him respond appropriately!

"Honey, it's okay to cry but you are all right. Let Mama pray for you. Hey, sweetie, think you'll be all right by the time you get married?" He laughs and nods his head, wipes his tears, and stands up. Then I think, *Whew! This time seems like I did okay. Give me wisdom, Lord!*

Bill's response would depend on what box he was in at the time. He likes to describe them as multiple-choice boxes/responses:

a). *Tough guy box:* No blood, no broken bones, and he's breathing means, "Okay, son, suck it up, you'll be all right!"

b). *Sympathetic dad box:* "Wow! That must hurt, son. Let Dad give ya a hug and help you up."

c). *Macho man:* This one doesn't include getting involved to help. He will simply let mom respond as he yells from the garage, "You okay, son? Sounds like it! Hey, come here and I'll show you the scar from when I ripped open my knee on a sprinkler head."

To Bill, it is an isolated incident but not to me. I attach all kinds of meaning to one small second in time. I instantly run all possible scenarios through my mind like a rapid fire computer. Maybe that's why studies say: During the first years of their lives, children tend to laugh and smile more at their fathers, but are more likely to turn to their mothers for reassurance when threatened or in distress.[1]

It appears this difference is by design. One study finds that girls who have high measures of male hormones show less maternal instincts—testosterone apparently contributes to the way a man responds.[2] The influence of hormones on the development of each gender is not yet fully understood, and researchers have not yet discovered the extent that inborn characteristics influence the way boys and girls are raised by their parents. What is obvious, however, is that boys and girls approach life differently. One study of boys and girls notes:

> At a physiological level, girls and boys were equally affected by the sight of the child smiling or crying. Their heart rate tended to slow down when it smiled, and they became physiologically aroused when they saw that it was crying. But it would have been impossible to tell that they shared the same gut reaction from the way that they behaved. The girls looked much more interested while the boys pretended to ignore the baby's distress, a sex difference which was much more marked among the older than the younger children.[3]

This same dichotomy continues as men and women become parents. Mom is usually the primary caregiver when the kids are young. To be sure, one of the reasons for this is the ability of mom to nurse her newborn child, ensuring a close, constant emotional bond. As kids grow, dad gets increasingly involved as he becomes more comfortable with their needs and feels more competent to meet them. When kids enter late adolescence, they tend to look to their dads for help in making the major decisions of life.

The Power of a Waffle

It can be discouraging to mom that the kids keep turning to dad for the major decisions when she has been there for *all* their ups and downs, broken bones and broken hearts, and a thousand other experiences they have since forgotten. The importance of mom is indisputable, but it appears that dad has an influence on his kids that mom cannot duplicate. In our experience working with families for the last 20 years, we have noticed that kids whose dads have been actively involved and aggressively interested in their lives are more confident and much more likely to make healthy decisions. Conversely, teens whose dads were absent or uninvolved are more insecure and make decisions that complicate their lives. In terms of future success, the discernment to recognize a good choice in a mate, and the ability to maintain emotional balance in life, dad is the difference!

When both parents are involved in child-rearing, their roles are not interchangeable. "Fathers tend to be more physical when they play with children, while mothers favour conventional games like peek-a-boo, and also provide them with more intellectual stimulation by reading to them or encouraging them to manipulate objects."[4] While children do tend to turn to mom for comfort and reassurance, dad's role is just as vital. A child's relationship with dad is the most important factor in determining how he or she will react to the rest of the world. For example, "an experiment carried out on six-month-old boys found that those who had most contact with their fathers were least disturbed when a stranger of either sex picked them up. Similarly, a recent American study shows that the less frequently babies of both sexes are dressed and bathed by their fathers, the longer they cry when they are left alone with an adult they don't know."[5]

In addition to making children more confident socially, fathers make a significant contribution in the intellectual development. "The rocking, talking and touching that fathers provide in response to their children's signals teaches a baby that it can affect other people by its actions, and encourages its intellectual curiosity. As a result, research shows that the more contact a child has with its father, the more advanced it is likely to be. This effect is more marked for boys, though other aspects of a father's behaviour can also have a direct effect on a daughter's intellectual development."[6]

The Influence of a Good Spaghetti Dinner

What does the care of a mother look like? It is easily recognizable. One study explains:

> Most mothers seem to have a standard way of touching their newborn babies, beginning with the arms and legs and then stroking the back and stomach. They also tend to hold their babies so that they can look into each other's eyes. When holding or feeding the baby, they bring its face to within about a foot of their own, which happens to be the distance at which a newborn baby's eyes focus best. More significantly, even adults without children consistently hold babies at a distance at which the baby's—though not necessarily their own—eyes are best in focus. Mothers also pitch their voices higher when talking to their babies, and we know (though mothers may not) that babies are more responsive to high-pitched sounds.[7]

God intends for children to respond to mom's voice. Mom plays a powerful role in the life of a child. Because she integrates life and emotionally connects to those closest to her, mom provides the first primary trust relationship with a child. The more bonded a child is to mom those first few weeks and months, the stronger his or her ability is to trust others.

Dr. Brenda Hunter, in her book *Where Have All the Mothers Gone*, examines studies by numerous specialists in the mother-child bond. Dr. Jack Raskin, child psychiatrist at Children's Orthopedic Hospital and at the University of Washington, states, "no psychological event is as important as the bonding that occurs between the mother and child during the first few moments of life."[8] Psychoanalyst John Bowlby points out that this attachment to mom is the "foundation stone of personality." Bowlby explains that the mother-child attachment is evident through childhood and only weakens as the teen years progress because more adults become important to the child.[9] There is a preponderance of evidence gathered since WW II that children who have been institutionalized because they have no mother, and children who are tossed from foster home to foster home, are at high risk for becoming permanently impaired. Maggie Scarf says that when this basic relationship is disturbed, and the mother is absent, especially during the first four to five years of life, "the child experiences acute psychological pain. This anguish has three distinct stages: protest, despair, and finally detachment. When the child reaches the last stage…he no longer cares. And if this separation from mother is too long, the process may never be reversed. Some children literally die from the absence of this protective and absorbing emotional bond."[10]

Is It Nature or Nurture?

Mom's influence is a gift that must be cultivated because this primary nurturing relationship isn't instantaneous. "Recent surveys have shown that only about half of women feel an immediate sense of love for their babies. Four out of ten first-time mothers recall that their predominant emotion on holding their baby for the first time was indifference. In the huge majority of cases, however, this is replaced by love and affection within a week of delivery, and it should be said that an early lack of affection is often linked to some understandable cause such as difficult labour, unusually large doses of pain-killers, or depression which existed before the child was born."[11] Though its causes are not well understood, postpartum depression can also be a contributing factor to the mother-child bond.

> The condition of post-natal depression, which affects a significant number of new mothers, is less well understood. Contrary to what many doctors believe, it does not seem to be caused by hormonal irregularities, and is not confined to the weeks after giving birth. It is unknown in most non-industrial societies, especially in those where long-established custom removes the need for parents to make decisions about how to rear their children. Post-natal depression may well be the price of individual freedom and responsibility in this aspect of living.[12]

Most moms and dads eventually make the adjustments that are necessary and find that life is enhanced by parenthood. One mother recently told me (Pam), "I am happier now that I have realized life is not all about me—in fact, it is rarely about me!"

Both mom and dad have to adjust to the change of lifestyle that accompanies the birth of a new baby. By accepting that you approach life differently, you can strategically help the transition along. Dad needs to create a new box that provides time for his kids and interest in being their dad. If he develops this box and spends time there, it will provide time for mom to rest and regroup. And mom will discover that she can continually add relationships to her life with the birth of each child. Her emotional capacity increases and her life gets fuller. While this is happening, she may assume that the box her husband has likewise expanded his emotional horizons. But he has simply added a box to the husband box. He still wants the husband box to get the same attention, and he still wants to go to easy boxes to destress. She will help immensely if she chooses not to get her feelings hurt if dad feels the need for a game of racquetball or a round of golf to get his equilibrium again.

A note of caution. Bill and I have seen a rise in the number of men and women bailing out on their families in these early years. The transition to parenthood is a natural one that is packed with responsibility, so it is easy to feel overwhelmed. The problem with running away from life is when you run away— YOU are still there—only to repeat the same negative patterns with more baggage. Transitions in life can seem overwhelming, parenthood especially, but transitions are normal. When you look back on these events, they will be some of your strongest memories.

Pam and I had the opportunity to build our home in California. It was a very grueling year as we did much of the work ourselves. In order to get our final permit so we could move into the house, we had to plant ice plant on the hills in the front and back yards along with a sprinkler system. I diligently worked to get the sprinkler system in so we could enjoy our new home. Thirty-eight sprinkler heads and two weeks later, the inspector signed off our final permit. We moved in and began to enjoy a well-deserved rest from the rigors of a year of construction.

Two months later, I was pulling into the driveway after a day's work when I witnessed a sprinkler head fly over the front windshield of my car. As I climbed out of my car and looked up at the hill from which the projectile had come, I noticed my two oldest boys and one of their friends holding baseball bats in their hands. They were practicing their golf swings by teeing off on my sprinkler heads! I have to admit that for a moment I forgot I was a pastor. All I could focus on was the anger that was boiling up in my heart as I dwelled on how disrespectful my kids were being as they destroyed part of my dream home.

"Raymond, you better go home," I said with a tone of doom in my voice. "Boys, you better go in the house before I do something we all regret."

My sons headed inside and disappeared. Pam realized after about half an hour that an eerie silence had descended on our home. She went and found the boys and asked them where I was.

"I think he is still outside," they sheepishly responded without wanting to get involved.

When Pam came out of the house she found me walking around the yard murmuring to myself, "I would rather have kids than sprinklers. I would rather have kids than sprinklers." It took me over an hour to convince myself that *I would rather have kids than sprinklers!*

Hints for Raising a Waffle

Because women are much more verbal than men, and because women can tap into their emotions easier than most men, one of the biggest favors you can do for a son is to raise his vocabulary, especially when it comes to expressing his emotion. One of our three sons, Zach, was especially nonverbal. His typical answers included vague responses such as, "I dun' know, okay, uh huh, whatever…" But more than anything he'd just shrug his shoulders when asked, "How do you feel?" "or "What's wrong, honey?"

Zach had a sensitive heart. He was the one to try to comfort a crying baby, the first one on the scene when a small toddler fell. He spotted the symptoms of my migraines before anyone else in my family, always asking if he could help me. But he couldn't express his own emotions, even though he could spot emotion in others. Knowing that his future wife would want more than grunts and moans, I went to the local teacher's supply store and bought a poster that had lines and lines of circles on it, each with a face that depicted a different emotional state. Under each was the word describing that feeling, like, "discouraged, stressed, pensive," etc. Then each time I would see Zach having a change in emotions, I would take him to the poster and ask him to point out how he was feeling. Of course, I had to give definitions and descriptions of the emotional words to aid him in making the appropriate choice. Later I discovered a magnet that had many of these faces on it with a movable frame that said "Today I feel…" So each day Zach would move the frame as he came in from school.

We began playing games to help him learn to express his emotions. I would ask questions like, "If how you are feeling right now was an animal, what animal would it be?"

At first, I'd get the typical "I dun' know." For example, when he was having a tough time with homework one night, I asked a multiple-choice question, "Is it like a bobcat that wants to attack or a kitten that is mad and cornered or a cheetah that wants to run away fast? Or is it something else?" I'd act out all the choices with full sound effects. "It's like the cheetah, Mom!" Zach would say excitedly.

"So you feel like running away?"

"Yeah, I guess so."

"Why do you want to run away, honey?"

"I dun' know."

"Is it because you don't want to do this? Or because you are afraid you aren't going to do it right or well? Or—"

"That's it, Mom. I don't think I can get it right."

The breakthrough for Zachery gave me the opportunity to explain to him that what Bill and I value most in him is when he tries his best. We have accepted that each person in our family will have different strengths and weaknesses. What we will applaud is when he is the best Zach he can be rather than trying to be perfect or like one of his brothers. We had told Zach this before, but this time he heard it.

Zach felt freed up emotionally and the homework struggle we'd been having nightly suddenly came to an end.

This technique proved so successful that I have added other questions, "What kind of car would you use to describe how you are feeling? What kind of food?" Sometimes I compare a current feeling with something he's gone through in the past. For example, one day when Zach was eight, he was taking piano lessons and he sat frozen on the piano bench. I walked through the living room and casually said, "Zach. Practice, buddy."

He just sat there. I went over and put my hand on his shoulder. "Here, play this one. I love this one." I flipped back to a very familiar tune that I knew he had mastered weeks before. He shook his head no.

I sat down on the bench next to him. "Zach, you can do this one. I know you can. You've done it lots before."

He shook his head, tears rolling down his cheeks. "Honey, what's wrong? What is it?"

Zach just sat frozen and silent, tears rolling down his face. "Zach, what is it? You can do this. Here, I'll do it with you." I placed my hand on his and lifted it to the keys. Zach violently pulled his hand back, slamming my hand hard against the wood of the bench.

"Zach! You could have hurt Mom or yourself. You don't have to practice right now, but you do have to practice sometime. What you do need to do is tell me what is going on in your head."

"I'm stupid!"

"You're not stupid. Why would you say that?"

"I'm stupid."

"Zach, I'm not going to argue with you. You know we don't allow that word. But what I want to know is why you are feeling like you are stupid?"

His shoulders shrugged. This went on for a few go-arounds. I was saying he wasn't stupid and Zach was shrugging his shoulders while he wiped his tears. I tried being compassionate, tough, and concerned. I even tried walking away and being as stubborn as he was being. "Fine, Zach, sit there. But you will sit there until you practice or until you tell me what's wrong and how you are feeling."

I glanced at the clock on the wall. What had once been a half-hour practice session had turned into an hour-and-a-half dead-end argument. I felt like I was beating my head on the wall of Zach's heart. I turned and walked back into the living room and sat down next to my small son. I turned him by the shoulders so we sat face to face. I took his chin and held it in my hand. "Zach, I'm going to be very serious right now. Someday you are going to grow up. You are a smart, talented young man that will someday have a job, get married, and have kids. If you shut down your emotions, if you won't share what is going on inside you, then your wife will always have her feelings hurt. Right now, my feelings are hurt because I thought you trusted me to help you with your feelings, but you won't share with me. Zach, if you grow up and won't talk to your wife or your kids, you will be very, very lonely. No one will really know what a great guy you are down here." I tapped on his chest. "Zach, let us into your heart."

He sobbed out loud. "But I will never be as good as Brock, so why should I try?"

"Is that what's going on? You think you have to be as good as your older brother at the piano? I don't even care if you end up playing the piano. We just have every son take piano for one year so they can be exposed to music. You never, ever have to compare yourself to either of your brothers. You can play any instrument you want. But one thing you cannot do, honey, is stuff your emotions, especially if you are feeling like this."

"Like a failure," he sighed.

"Oh, honey," I said as I wrapped my arms around him, "you will never be a failure as long as you share the wonderful Zach that's in here." I tapped on his heart again. "You don't have to be anyone other than yourself. Promise me, anytime you are feeling frozen you will tell me. To make it easy, if you are frozen because you are feeling like you might fail just call it your *piano* feeling, okay?"

"Okay, Mom."

Still to this day, six years later, Zach will whisper to me, "Mom, pray for me. I have that piano feeling again." His confidence has grown and he rarely gets that "piano feeling," but when he does, he now has the ability to articulate exactly what it is. Recently he said, "Mom, I am excited about going to high school. I think I would like to be someone who helps other people, you know, like Dad does—as a counselor. A Christian counselor or maybe a youth pastor. I want to help people process their emotions and feelings. I want to help them so they don't feel afraid of life. Mom, they have classes for that in high school, don't they?"

Hints for Understanding Your Noodling Daughter

The best thing you can do for your daughter is patiently listen to her and touch her often. I (Pam) was always amazed when my next-door neighbor, Shannon, would come over to play with our youngest son, Caleb. Shannon chatted and chatted, following me from room to room, barely stopping to breathe. As we are raising three boys, I am not used to that many words in one day. I kind of liked it, but I was definitely not in listening shape for that many words.

Because we have not raised a daughter, we can only talk with you about what we have seen in the lives of young ladies that have been a part of our ministry over the past two decades. What is obvious from our experience is that girls need to talk through their lives. They process life verbally. They figure out what good friends are like by talking about their experiences with their parents. They discover how to respond to hurts and disappointments by talking through the experiences with their parents. They learn to guide their emotions in life by talking them through with their parents. If their parents are not available to talk with them, the girls don't stop talking. They just turn their conversations to peers or other trusted adults. Other adult attention is not as effective because they do not have the same emotional bond as with mom and dad. The interest of peers is not as effective because they are not mature enough to give healthy insight.

The other interesting corollary to listening is the importance of physical touch and daughters. Kind, encouraging, appropriate touching releases endorphins in the body. Endorphins are chemicals in the human body that make people "feel" better. It is as if they are one of God's rewards for doing the right thing. When a daughter has loving, respectful physical contact with her parents, she "feels" better about whatever she is doing. By demonstrating consistent affection, parents help their daughters associate good feelings with the activities of life. When endorphins are released during conversation, daughters associate conversation with feeling good. When making decisions is accompanied by reassuring touches to the arm or hand, she associates decision-making with feeling good. When conflict is worked through and it concludes with being able to sit in your lap and cuddle for a little while, even conflict resolution will be associated with feeling good. Because your daughter will relate all that happens in her life to the emotional state she was in at the time, you do her a great favor when you make physical affection a consistent part of her life.

One parent-child expert has captured the essence of successful parenting with these words, "the child should spend a substantial amount of time with somebody who's crazy about him."[13]

Differences in Parenting

God has made you a team in parenting your children. Neither of you has the full perspective, and together you will be better for your kids than you could be on your own. This is great news, but it can also create tension because there are times you will just not see eye to eye. When that happens, we try to remind ourselves that we both have valuable insight into our sons. I (Pam) can see the connections between all the factors in our kids' lives. As a result, sometimes I have the best answer because Bill will be too narrow in his perspective. But sometimes Bill has the advantage over me because, well, he is one of them! I sometimes get overwhelmed with what *might* happen and will say no just because I don't have control of the situation.

We reached a new plateau in our parenting journey when our oldest son started driving. Not long ago, he approached Bill while I was out of town and asked him, "Dad, my friend Josh is going to have a party at his house after practice on Friday. It is just a few of his friends. Can I drive myself and go?"

If I had been the one who was home, I am not sure we would have had a reasonable conversation, but Bill was able to get into the box with Brock. He asked him, "Well, Brock, you know our concerns. Is there going to be a responsible parent there? What is the plan if it gets out of hand?"

Bill knew that Brock would be focused on the night as a single event. I, on the other hand, would have brought up the danger of driving, the hazards of alcohol and drugs, and the impact of peer pressure on teenagers. I would have wanted absolute certainty that none of those things would be a problem. Bill was able to keep it simple but effective.

Brock explained that Josh's mom was going to be there. He anticipated our concern about alcohol and said the only thing to drink would be soft drinks. Then he outlined what he would do if upperclassmen crashed the party. Because he covered the box, Bill let him go.

It turns out some seniors did show up with a keg of beer and tried to take over the party. Brock called Bill to explain he was leaving and would be home in a few minutes. He also asked if his friends could come to our house and keep having fun. When Bill said they could, Brock asked if he could come get them because our 16-year-old son's license only allowed him to drive alone, and he was going to respect it. While they were still on the phone, Brock was able to arrange for rides and the night ended successfully.

Looking back, I am glad Bill was there to handle that one, because I think I would have made too much out of it and frustrated my son. Instead, I am now even more proud of both my son and his dad.

It's Not Just a Cookie

It is generally easier for the parent of the same sex to understand the needs of a particular child, but both sides are still needed. During Brock's freshman year, he was captain of the JV men's volleyball team at his high school. One day I picked him up from practice and noticed that he was upset. Bill and I have stressed anger management and self-control with our boys their entire life, so it is rare when any of them get carried away with visible actions of anger. But Brock got in the car and with a clenched fist slammed his leg and said, "I am so mad!" He went on to explain that there was a contest in practice where two players were matched up into teams and the winning team won a big chocolate chip cookie. Seems Brock, the best player on the team, was paired with a poor player and he lost the contest.

I tried my mother's logic first, "Honey, you know it was just a motivation tool of the coach. He still knows you are a great volleyball player."

"Mom, I know coach knows I am a committed player. It's not that."

"Well, you aren't letting this attack your self-image as a player are you? It was just a game."

"Just a game!" Now Brock was agitated at me! "Mom, you just don't get it!"

"Well, tell me then!"

"I wanted to win."

"Honey, I'll get you a cookie!"

"Mom! It's not about the cookie!"

"Then what is it about? Your fragile male ego?"

Brock shot me a glare and I knew I was right—and it was the wrong thing to say! The next day I thought I would cheer Brock up, so I brought him a chocolate chip cookie after practice with a card that said, "I think you're a winner!"

Brock opened the card and said, "Mom, thank you so much. Your heart is in the right place, but you still don't get it. Ask Dad about it. I think he could explain it better. I don't want to hurt your feelings. Thanks for the cookie, Mom."

So I asked Bill after explaining the entire cookie incident.

"Pam, it *was* about ego. For a teen boy, winning is everything. Winning reflects their self-image, and they are always jockeying to be at the top of the pile. Brock, being a good athlete, saw a chance to be recognized as a winner and he wanted it!"

"But it was just a cookie!" I said in frustration. "The coach and all the players already know Brock is the best on the team. Brock even knows it. What is all the fuss over a cookie?"

"It's not the cookie—it's the *winning* of the cookie. He probably would have even given the cookie away."

"So should I be worried about Brock being angry that he didn't win the cookie? He looked really steamed. You should have seen him!"

"I'll talk with him again and remind him of our standards of self-control, but you don't have anything to worry about. He's normal. He has terrific self-control and composure on and off the field, so I'm sure even Brock has realized he overreacted. And you should expect to see him that competitive again. He gives 110 percent and I wouldn't want to change that. It's cookies now—but it'll be bonuses and perks later on in business."

The realization suddenly hit me. "You're right. I want him to fight for what's right. I don't want to take the heart out of him. When he gets married and things get tough, I want that competitive spirit to kick in and help him fight for his marriage and family. When college comes and life isn't handed to him on a silver platter, I want him to be assertive and motivated."

"Now you're getting it."

I knew Bill was right, but I also knew that if it was up to him, the impact of this event would be over. The box had been visited, the problem had been solved, and the door was shut. I, however, could sense that chocolate chip cookies were going to have special meaning for Brock and me for the rest of our lives.

I shared my conversation with Bill the next day with Brock.

"Mom, you're right in that I need to control my temper—always. But Dad was right on in why I wanted the cookie. I want to win in life and Dad is right, I want to channel that winning spirit into things that are good for my future and my future family."

"I'll make you a deal, Brock."

"What?"

"You keep competing 100 percent but keep self-control. And I'll keep buying you chocolate chip cookies and cheering you on—okay?"

"Deal, Mom. Thanks!"

Parenting is a team sport. When you put your efforts together and invest your uniqueness into your child, he or she can run to win!

True, personal stories from good friends learning about the surprises and joy of parenting:

Six-year-old Emily came home from school one day, and declared to her mother in a disgusted tone, "I never want to have kids. To get children you have to have sex!"

Her mother, shocked that her youngest of four children even was aware of the facts of life, let out an audible gasp.

Emily saw the shocked look on her mother's face and said, "What? You didn't know?"

▲ ▲ ▲

Some friends of ours adopted their two children. One day after their young son was made aware of the facts of life, he told his teacher, "Whew! I'm glad I'm adopted so my parents never had to do that!"

Waffles and Spaghetti
Meeting Each Other's
Key Needs

Sauce or Syrup?

"What it means to be female or male, what it's like to talk to someone of the other (or the same) [sex], are questions whose answers touch people where they live, and when a nerve is touched, people howl." [1]

There are two things that I (Bill) tell people to eliminate from heterosexual relationships. The first is a question that couples seem to have an insatiable appetite for. It is the question "Why?" It comes in a myriad of forms:

"Why do you feel that way?"

"Why are you thinking that?"

"Why do you think you had that reaction?"

"Why are you so upset?"

"Why can't you just accept that this is the way it is?"

The reason I want to ask "Why?" is that I don't understand what is going on with the one I love. I guess I keep hoping I am going to someday get a reasonable answer. But the answer will never come. The question I am actually asking is, "Why do you have emotions?" We all have emotions, and though they are not logical, they motivate everything we love and everything we do. So the answer to the "why" question is "I am emotional." This is why emotional intimacy is so important to a healthy marriage.

The other is a statement that permeates our relationships: "I understand." It too comes in various forms:

"I understand how you feel."

"I understand what you're thinking."

"I understand how upset you must be right now."

"I understand your hurt."

"I understand how happy you are right now."

These sound like compassionate, caring, even insightful statements, but in reality they are attempts to stop the conversation. We get tired of listening and want to start sharing our own thoughts, so we interrupt with, "I understand."

The intention is definitely sincere, but the problem is we can never truly understand each other. We tell men every chance we get that the day they will understand their wives is the first day they have a menstrual period. And we tell women that the day they will understand their husbands is the day they experience an aggressive rush of testosterone throughout their body. But don't lose hope—even though you may never fully *understand* your spouse, you can *discover* him or her in an ongoing adventure of love.

Questions of Security

So what are we going to discover about each other that is different than what we experience? Men are going to discover that their wives are driven to experience security. Security is your wife's most pervasive need. She longs to know that life with you is safe. She wants to be assured of physical safety, financial safety, social safety, and emotional safety. She doesn't mean to be unreasonable about this, but it is a constant need for her to know she is secure with you. One way this can be accomplished in her heart is through the gift of encouraging words.

We discovered the power of encouraging words while on our honeymoon, I (Pam) had just stepped from the shower and was looking into the mirror. I began to criticize my body. Bill was sitting on the bed, admiring his new wife. As I would comment on an area I thought needed improving, Bill began to panic. He was afraid I would continue to point out my shortcomings, then get depressed, and sex would be out of the question! I went on for a few minutes until he could stand it no longer. He was angry that I would put down his choice of a wife. I was not only tearing myself down but undermining Bill's taste. Instead of saying something in anger, he prayed, "God, I could do a better job than that mirror!"

He stood up, wrapped his arms around me, and told me to look straight into his eyes. He very seriously and very lovingly said, "I will be your mirror. My eyes will reflect your beauty. You are beautiful, Pamela. You are perfect, and if you ever doubt it, come stand before me. The mirror of my eyes will tell you the true story. You are perfect for me. If I have to throw away every mirror in the house to get you to believe me, I will! From now on, let me be your mirror!"

For more than 21 years, Bill has reflected to me my worth and value from God's point of view.

In "The Mirror," a song written about this moment for our twenty-fifth wedding anniversary by Boomer and Lisa Reiff, there is this line:

> And now she looks back on her life—at all the years that
> have come and gone—and she knows the gift he gave
> that day became the ground she's walked upon.

And it has. Bill's gift of encouraging words met a deep security need and the level of trust I gained for him that day went through the roof. He's still earning romance points for that moment and it happened over 27 years ago now!

To build confidence that she is safe, a woman continually asks a series of questions in her heart to confirm that her security is intact. To put it into perspective, your wife needs to have her security met as often as you would like to have sex with her.

Question 1: Am I More Important Than Our Money?

She knows that money is important, and she wants your family to be successful, but inside her heart she needs to know that you are not so consumed with making and managing money that you lose sight of who she is. As long as she knows that you consider her more valuable than your cash flow she will be reasonable and cooperative in your financial decisions. If, however, she feels she needs to compete with money for your attention, she will make sure that money takes second place.

Many of you are asking, "Why does she do this?" Let me remind you this is an emotional need and emotions do not run on logic. They are designed to be expressed, and that is really all they do. When emotional needs come to the surface, they demand expression and often complicate our lives. The key is to acknowledge them with compassion. When the emotional needs of our lives are acknowledged and compassionately accepted, they find their fulfillment and soften.

Amy illustrates how this works from her own experience. "I lost my ring. My husband helped me look for it for six hours. We looked everywhere but couldn't find it! The center stone of the ring was from his mother's wedding ring. I was devastated! He went to bed. I sat in the living room and cried.

"He finally noticed I was missing and came to look for me. He sat down beside me, took my hands in his, and said, 'Amy, I just want you to know that whatever happens, things are just things and I love you anyway.' All of a sudden something told me to look under the sofa—again. There was the ring!"

Question 1 reveals itself in romance on a regular basis. When a man deliberately spends money on his wife to communicate to her that she is valuable to him, he reaches straight to her heart. When a wife feels like she is a financial priority to her husband, her heart moves closer to him.

Mary and her husband discovered the joy of this recently. "Day after day, when I was pregnant, I lowered myself into my recliner as only a pregnant woman can. One night during my ninth month, we had company come visit. In the middle of conversation, my husband asked me, 'Honey, can you get me a glass of water?' I had just lowered myself into the recliner! He was sitting comfortably in a chair, but since we had guests, I got up thinking, *I'll talk to him later! *!#*!* There in the cabinet, next to the glasses, was a pair of sapphire earrings that I had admired earlier!"

Question 2: Are You Being Sincere?

"Pam, you are beautiful. I knew it when I married you, and I am even more convinced now that there is no one on earth as attractive as you." I thought I was being pretty smooth with those words. I had noticed that Pam was feeling self-conscious about herself during the year after the birth of our third son. I was still very much in love with her, and I wanted her to know that I still thought she was a pretty woman.

Her response was, "You are just doing this because you have to. You don't really mean it."

It drives me crazy when she does this. Even if I am not being sincere, I want my words to soften her heart and draw her to me. She, on the other hand, goes through a very different process than I do. Because everything in her life is connected to everything else, trust is a never-ending pursuit. When Pam trusts me, she trusts me with everything. When she opens her heart in one area, all the other areas of her life feel the need to open up also. If she is confident that I am sincere in my devotion and compliments, she feels that it is safe to trust me. If she thinks I am just flattering her with my words, she will be reluctant to trust me emotionally because she feels she is setting herself up to be hurt.

I don't believe that women have this struggle intentionally. They are often aware that they are overstating the need for their husbands to be sincere, but they can't turn it off until they are confident they are getting responses from the heart.

Listen to the words of Jan. "I come from a family with a history of over 50 divorces. My husband's parents just celebrated 62 years together. Thirty-three years ago, when we were first married, I said something sharp to him. He sensed my insecurity, and he said, 'There is nothing you can do to make me quit loving you!' I suddenly realized I had been trying to make him quit loving me so the pain would be over sooner. His words cemented my trust in him!"

Sincerity is not just about words, however. The gifts you give also must be delivered with sincerity, and it is often when you have the least money that your wife will believe you have the most sincerity.

At one of Pam's women's conferences a lady named Mikki bragged about her husband's sincerity. "Once when we were really low on money my husband drew a picture of a rose on a piece of paper and gave it to me. I keep that favorite flower in my Bible."

Question 3: Do You Notice Me?

Every wife wants to know that her husband thinks about her, likes to be with her, and notices the newness in her life. This is one of the reasons that conversation is important to your wife. She wants to know if you think her words are important and attractive. She wants to know that you are interested in the way she thinks and that you want to share with her the way you think. A wise husband schedules regular time just to visit with his wife.

The other obvious way this question manifests itself is in the way your wife fishes for compliments.

"Do you notice anything different about me, honey?"

Doesn't this question send chills up and down your spine?

I had the opportunity to crash and burn on this recently. Pam made an appointment to get her hair cut and weaved. She had announced this appointment a number of times in the days leading up to the appointment, but in typical male fashion I was in a box that did not include noticing.

She was sure I would love it and would swoon over her when she came home. She was bouncing around the house that night anticipating my weak knees when I saw her dazzling beauty recently enhanced by her new hairstyle. I vaguely noticed that night something was different but my instincts were stuck in neutral. Pam transitioned from bouncing to focusing on the responsibility of her life.

I didn't say anything—for five days! Then she finally asked, "Haven't you noticed anything different?"

I took a very studious look at her and triumphantly announced, "Pam, your hair looks great!"

Her response was, "Oh, you finally noticed. Thanks, Bill! It is good to have you back."

I probably would be harder on myself for my shortsightedness if Pam and I weren't in such good company. We even see great people in the Bible fishing for compliments. In the Song of Songs 2:1,2 King Solomon's bride, the Shulamite, prods him with the following words, "I am a rose of Sharon, a lily of the valleys."

The rose of Sharon and the lily of the valley were the most common flowers growing on the hills around her parents' farm. What she is saying is, "I am just a plain country girl. There is nothing special about me. How could you as a king choose someone like me who lacks any real beauty?" To say the least, she is feeling insecure. If Solomon agrees with her, he might as well make reservations for the doghouse!

But his response is remarkable when he says, "Like a lily among thorns is my darling among the maidens" (verse 2). Oh, my goodness, how did he come up with that one on the spur of the moment? He looked her in the eyes and said, "Compared to you, all the other women in the world are thorns and you are the single flower!"

We know her heart melted because her response is, "Like an apple tree among the trees of the forest is my lover among the young men" (verse 3). When is the last time you saw an apple tree in the forest? She is letting him know that there has never been a man like him before because he hit the target of her heart dead center.

Question 4: Am I More Important Than Your Sleep?

It was the last day of our honeymoon, and we were experiencing what I (Bill) believed to be the best of all possible worlds. We were in Lake Tahoe enjoying the newness of our marriage. We had been introduced to the guilt-free thrills of physical intimacy between a husband and wife. The only downside was we were out of money. But we were traveling the next morning to Pam's relatives to celebrate Christmas, and we knew there was money waiting for us there. We needed to get up very early to drive to Reno to catch our flight to Idaho, so I figured we should go to bed early enough to get a good night's sleep. This seemed very reasonable to me, but I forgot to ask Pam if that was what she had in mind.

The anticipation of this being the last night of our honeymoon led to a great time of sexual intimacy. What happened next was the beginning of new education for me. I have since learned that good sex winds women up—and they stay wound up for a long time. During the next three hours, I heard about every boyfriend she had ever had in life. The first was when Pam was eight years old and, as far as I could tell, there was not a year in her life when she didn't have a special relationship. She told me she wanted to share every detail of her life with me. She wanted me to know everything. As a young, idealistic husband I concurred and thought it would actually be possible to listen to Pam with the same level of attention with which she was sharing herself.

I held my own for the first hour. I became a little restless during the second hour. The third hour was a disaster. In the middle of a sentence I started to doze off, but I caught myself in time to shift my body and find the alertness to continue listening without her realizing I was losing it. Some time after that I did it. I fell fast asleep while she was baring her soul. I was awakened to a "heartquake" that registered 3.5 on our bed.

Pam was convulsively sobbing, murmuring, "I thought you loved me. How could you fall asleep on me? Am I really that boring?"

I thought these were honest questions! I thought Pam really wanted an answer to what she asked, so I sat up in bed, looked her in the eyes, and said, "I really do love you. I am so sorry for falling asleep. Go ahead and finish. I will listen to you talk about the men who came before me but couldn't capture your heart."

Pam pushed the issue, "You don't really want to hear it. You are just saying you will listen because you have to."

With a little bit of desperation in my voice, I reassured her, "No, I really want to know. Every detail of your life is important to me."

"Do you really mean it?"

"Yes, Pam. I really mean it!"

"Okay," she said with a glint in her eye, "I want to tell you about the country western songs I listened to growing up." Then she started singing!

I had been had. Here I was trying to address Pam's stated concern, and I totally missed the real issue. The concern that was truly on her heart was, "Bill, am I more important to you than your sleep? Are you willing to be tired to show me that I have first place in your heart?"

I (Pam) saw that Bill passed this test with flying colors so he hasn't had to listen to any more renditions of Tammy Wynette since then!

Question 5: Do You Notice Other Women?

This is one of the hardest to recognize and respond to strategically. Your wife will ask you, "What do you think of that woman's haircut?"

At times the right answer is "What woman?" as if you don't know that any other woman exists. During these times your wife will be touched by your dedicated affection and feel closer to you for protecting her unique value in your life. Other times, she will criticize you for being blind to her cosmetic priorities and will give you the cold shoulder.

At other times the right answer is "Yes, I did. I think her haircut is cute. I even think you might look good in a style like that." One time she will be impressed that you would think about what would look good on her. The next time she will be offended you even noticed that other women had hair.

This question applies to noticing body types, clothing styles, modesty, and attitudes. We are required to be aware of the ploys and practices of women without really noticing that there are other women in the world. We need to treat all women with respect but only treat our wives with interest. You are supposed to notice that your wife is the most beautiful of all women without ever comparing her to another woman.

Questions of Simplicity

Women ask questions of security because their entire life is connected. Everything impacts everything else, so she is more prone to feel that things are out of control. Men have a corresponding characteristic in their lives. Because men compartmentalize life and have a problem-solving bent, they are drawn to the boxes where they think they can succeed. In fact, men only like to go to boxes where they can perform well. If he is good at communication, he likes that box. If he is not good at conversation, he prefers to avoid it. If he is good at making money, he gives his career lots of attention. If he is good at projects, he fills his life with projects. If he is lazy, he will look for ways to be lazy, and so on.

As a result of this pursuit of success, men like to keep life as simple as possible. The simpler life is, the fewer boxes he has to deal with. It is an emotional need in his life to seek simplicity. When things get complicated, he becomes demotivated and begins to detach himself from some of the boxes in life so he can simplify life to a level he can deal with. A wise wife helps her husband have a simple approach to life.

What are the questions men ask to keep their lives simple enough to succeed?

Question 1: Is Life with You Going to Be Filled with Admiration?

Because men love to succeed, they drink up compliments the way babies devour milk. The cousin to compliments is flirting. When a woman flirts with a man, the box he happens to be in at the moment ignites with enthusiasm. She may think she is playing a game, but he knows that the way to a man's heart is not food, it is flirting. Food fills his stomach, but compliments from the woman he loves fills his soul with confidence.

Think about it. One of the most common phrases in our world today is "You the man!" Men love to hear it and say it to one another. It makes them laugh and stand a little taller.

After more than two decades of being married to the same woman, I am still amazed at how her compliments energize me and, conversely, how her negative assessments of my life set me back. The two most obvious areas where I see this work consistently are in my preaching and in our dating life.

When I am finished with a Sunday service and Pam and I get a chance to talk, I still have a nagging wish that she will tell me I was great. When she gets a twinkle in her eye and says I delivered a sermon that is going to help a lot of people, I get a brand new lease on life. I feel physically lighter, I have more energy, my confidence in my abilities in other areas grows, and I think I look better. I know this an irrational response to her words, and yet it happens every time.

When, on the other hand, she picks out a part of the sermon and critiques it, I instantly go into recovery mode. In some ways, I am glad she can be honest and point out areas I can improve in. But in other ways, I am devastated—I feel physically heavier, everything in life seems more complicated, and I feel as though the entire morning was a failure. It takes me most of the afternoon to recover and get back to the place emotionally where I believe Pam didn't intentionally hurt me with the statements she made. I know this is an unfair burden to put on her, but I have not found a way to stop it, even after years of discipline and concentrated effort to change my reaction.

I have come to the conclusion that God made each man to be responsive to the words of his wife. Her compliments give him confidence, her flirting makes him feel sexy, her suggestions motivate him to change.

Another preacher had just finished his sermon, and he was greeting people at the door as they were leaving to enter their cars and head to lunch. One young lady in the congregation enthusiastically shook his hand and while holding on to it said to him, "Pastor, I believe you are one of the truly great preachers in our country."

On the drive home, his wife noticed that he was introspective with a rather contented smile on his face. She couldn't help but ask. He explained to her what had happened and what the young lady in the congregation had said.

The two of them rode in silence for another 15 minutes when she asked him, "What are you thinking?"

He hesitated, broke out in a sly smile, and said, "I was just wondering how many truly great preachers there are in this country."

She took a quick look at him, leaned over, and whispered in his ear, "One less than you think." Ouch!

Question 2: Is Life with You Going to Be Free from Complications?

Men are drawn to success like moths to the light. They love to be thought of as heroes, and they love to do the things they are good at. As a result, they sometimes become overwhelmed when life gets too complicated. This will usually cause tension for a married couple because while the man is focused on the areas he can succeed at, his wife is processing their entire life. She sees her needs, the kid's needs, the financial needs, the vacation plans, and her hope for their next date all at the same time. While he is trying to simplify matters, she is feeling that he is neglecting important areas of their life. There are a number of things a wife can do that will provide her husband some of the simplicity he craves.

Avoid unrealistic expectations. It is natural for a man to want to please his wife. He likes it when she is happy with his input and performance. He feels very good about himself when she smiles at him and says thanks. Her appreciation motivates him more intensely than he ever wants her to understand. The problem is that it is also natural for his wife to depend on him for the things she can't do. If her expectations are doable and there is realistic time to get it done, he will remain motivated to make life easier for her. If, on the other hand, her expectations are beyond his ability, his available time, or his financial potential, he instantly feels like a failure and loses motivation to do anything she has asked of him.

Avoid impossible schedule commitments. Most men are more than willing to let their wives plan their social calendars and watch over the family schedule. The average man gets overwhelmed by the variety of activities and the deluge of directions his family is running. He admires his wife's ability to somehow keep track of everyone and to maintain the same level of enthusiasm for each member's activities, but he knows he could never do the same. Most men trust their wives with this important area of life, but they secretly hope she has some limit. He desperately prays that she will know when to say no in their schedule because once the schedule gets constant, he will think he is losing control of his life and he will react. He may become angry, stubborn, withdrawn, or depressed.

Clue him in to unreasonable arguments. Men like to solve problems. Each man enjoys being an expert in a few areas of life, and he loves to be asked for his input. He falls into this problem-solving mode as easily as a new car starts when you turn the ignition key. When an argument starts between a man and a woman, he immediately assumes the problem-solving role. This is a great trait when the couple is looking for a logical answer to a problem, but how about when the argument is not logical? When emotions have built up and are being released and the argument is simply for the purpose of releasing emotional energy, there is no answer because there is no real problem. Often she just wants to talk through their life because there are more emotions running through her than she can control. If he will listen calmly, she will release the emotions and reconnect to the stability of her life. If he will not listen calmly but works hard to finish the conversation with questions such as, "What is the bottom line? Is there a point to this conversation?" the emotional energy will turn into an argument. The turmoil will then continue until the emotional pressure has been released.

Because men fall into this role so easily, it is helpful for him if his wife clues him in before they start talking. If she says to him, "Honey, I can tell I am pretty emotional, and I just need you to listen to me," he knows how to succeed and he will be more willing to interact. If she assumes he understands her needs and she just starts talking, he will assume there is a problem. He will start to form answers, he will miss the point, and he will become confused by her anger at his sincere attempts to help her and the turmoil will intensify.

Do your best to make your home a place to relax. Men need easy boxes to relax in. They are a little like rechargeable batteries. When you put a battery into a flashlight or some other electronic device, it wears down as it powers the device. When it wears down, it needs to be put in the charger. While it is in the charger, it appears to be doing nothing. It is not active and it is not working to make anything happen. But it is getting recharged. When men produce in life, they wear down. When men engage in conversation, they wear down. When men dispense advice, they wear down. As a result, they need to recharge, and it often frustrates most wives to watch this happen. The best place for a man to relax is at home, but if home is not available as an easy box, he will find another place to recharge his batteries.

Question 3: Is Life with You Going to Be Sexual?

Men don't set out to be unreasonable about sex with their wives, but they often find themselves sexually restless whenever they are together. She walks by and he notices the way her hips move. She smiles at him and he instantly feels sexy. He walks into the bedroom while she is changing her clothes, and he immediately thinks, *this might be a great opportunity.* All of us men know that this kind of thinking is unreasonable, and we even accept that we shouldn't be this way, but none of us are very good at it.

It is a strange area of life for men. Men pride themselves in being logical and focused on productivity. They like to make sense and they long for simple things. Alongside this desire is a man's sex drive which is in constant activation. As time passes since his last sexual encounter, he gets more and more focused on thoughts about sex. His wife gets prettier with each passing day. Every one of her features becomes more distinct and attractive. He finds himself thinking about her no matter what he is doing. As his desire intensifies, everything becomes a distraction, and he becomes unreasonably anxious to be intimate with her. If a satisfying sexual encounter is engaged in, all of life changes. He is able to focus on the daily things of life, and his entire being settles down. If the hope of sex is rejected, he finds himself irritated and will struggle with being angry. He tells himself this is crazy, but nothing he tries removes the tension except sex. As a result, men are embarrassingly in need of their wives' sexual attention.

Question 4: Is Life with You Going to Be Cooperative?

When men bring up a topic for conversation, they actually intend to talk about that topic. So when a husband tells his wife they need to talk about the budget, he wants to talk about the budget. If they talk through their money issues and a decision is made, the husband immediately assumes this decision is solid. If his wife, however, was merely exploring her emotions *about* the budget rather than deciding *on* the budget, she may find herself not sticking to the conclusions of their discussion.

Financial cooperation also becomes an emotional issue for men when it deals with his paycheck. Most men do not feel they make enough money and are consistently bothered by it. If he is working hard though, he will be hoping that his wife will be understanding and that they will live within their means. If she spends money according to her perception of their needs rather than according to their income, he will not only get frustrated with her but he will also feel like a failure.

I have seen many men perform well below their potential because of their wives' lack of cooperation. Steve started out working as a plumber's helper. The salary was not large but the training was good, and he thought he would make a career of it. But while he was getting his training his new wife, Sandy, seemed to always be unhappy with his choice. She made comments such as, "All you want to be is a plumber? How will we ever own an expensive home if you work with your hands?"

Steve almost welcomed the words because he really didn't like working with his hands and would rather work in an office. He began developing his own business as an insurance agent. He enjoyed networking with people and found satisfaction in providing products that protected their investments. The hours were long and the income was slow in developing, but he believed that with time he could effectively provide for his family. But Sandy kept nagging him, complaining that he wasn't making enough money. He tried to assure her that with time everything would work out, but she kept riding him.

I am sure she was just trying to look out for the family needs as she understood them, but he finally concluded that no matter what he did, she would not be happy. He was working long, hard hours and was getting tired of it. He finally decided that he should just get a 40-hour-per-week job that would at least lower the stress level of his life. He has now worked for a drafting company for the last 20 years, adequately providing for his family in a very predictable job. She is still disappointed and so is he, but he justifies it by reminding himself that at least his stress level is manageable.

Question 5: Is Life with You Going to Be Lived in the Present?

Because men like to live in one box at a time, they tend to focus on the present. They don't remember details of their past as readily as women because they don't create as many emotional attachments to the events of their past. Men want to preserve the dignity of the present.

First, a man hopes the past won't haunt his current relationship. Every man makes mistakes. He puts his foot in his mouth and offends his lover. He makes poor financial decisions and sets the family back. He fails to accept the security needs of his wife and makes her feel uncomfortably vulnerable. If his wife continues to bring these up after he learns his lesson and apologizes, he will think he lives in the shadow of failure.

Related to this are hurts his wife carries because of unhealthy relationships in her past. No man wants to pay for the mistakes of another man. Judy was molested by her uncle when she was seven years old. When her oldest daughter turned seven, the memories overtook her like a flood. She struggled with depression and panic. She was angry and grew overprotective of her two girls. Peter could understand these reactions, but he couldn't understand why she quit trusting him. He had been a good husband and a dedicated father, and now she was pushing him away. He felt like he was paying for the mistakes of her uncle and he was angry. He wanted to be on her side, but he was being treated like the enemy.

Anne was excited about dating when she became a teenager. She had thoughts of handsome young men treating her with respect and hosting her on many fun activities. She didn't start dating until she was eighteen, but she wishes she had waited even longer. The second young man she went out with forced himself on her sexually and would have nothing to do with her afterward. She didn't quit dating altogether, but she was very guarded from that day on. Amazingly, her overstated commitment to safety betrayed her and attracted a man who was intent on conquering her fear. He convinced her that he was considerate and respectful but things changed quickly when she said yes to him. He, too, forced himself on her.

She finally met Alex and fell in love. He turned out to be the genuine article, and they have a healthy, growing marriage. But Alex lives in frustration because there is some normal sexual activity that is off limits because it brings up painful memories. He longs to love her completely, but he has to hold back because of other men in her past. He continues to be considerate of her needs while he feels ripped off by what happened to her. Fortunately, she is courageously growing in her ability to forgive those men and trust Alex. Every step she takes draws Alex's heart closer to her.

Another interesting way that men long for the present is seen in the growth of responsibility. As the family life progresses, responsibility gets larger. With added responsibility, men want the expectations placed on them to change.

When Pam and I were newlyweds, I was able to give her my undivided attention. She was fun to be with and our life was very undemanding. I lavished her with words, simple gifts, and lots of time. For the first four years of our life together, it was easy to keep this up. Then we started having kids.

With each child, our schedule became more complicated and our financial needs grew. As a result, my commitment to my career grew. I needed Pam to be proud of my pursuits and applaud my productivity. At the same time, my opportunity to lavish her with attention was diminishing. More work hours meant less time with her. My children's needs were stealing time and energy away from Pam. If she had continued to expect the same romantic overtures from me that I was able to give early on, I would have become very frustrated. Because Pam broadened her acceptance of my contribution to her life to include the big picture of what I was doing, I have continued to fall even deeper in love with her.

Men long for success in the same way that women long for security. Men want to do everything they can succeed in and very little of what they fall short in. They are attracted to everything their wives do that makes them feel successful. Women want to feel safe in all areas of their lives and they are attracted to everything their husbands do to make them feel secure. When things get tense in your relationship, see if the underlying issue is one of security or simplicity. It may save you time and trauma because you will go to the core of the issue and give the gift of security and simplicity.

The Most Important Skill

Probably the most important skill you can develop as a couple in the pursuit of a great relationship is friendship. In a practical sense, friendships develop as you increase your knowledge of each other and then embrace that knowledge as a valuable asset in your life. Disclosing yourself to another individual is a sensitive pursuit. We all long for it because if someone else knows what we are all about and values the strange as well as the sensible about us, we feel a remarkable sense of intimacy with that person. Couples who deliberately promote their friendship understand the formula for success.

It goes without saying that true intimacy involves risk—a risk to open ourselves up and share; a risk to connect our life to another and share; a risk to care, to cherish, to accept one another; and a huge risk to sacrifice and serve. Where does this strength and courage to plunge in and risk to build a relationship come from? It is a strength that really needs to be more than any one human person can carry off—it is best carried out when a person taps into supernatural strength, the strength God can give to a relationship. He is able to help you build an incredible relationship with your spouse because he created him or her. God is able to help you to reveal yourself to your spouse which will build intimacy, he can help you understand yourself, and he can help you communicate this information to the one you love, again because he created you. He is not surprised that men are like waffles and women are like spaghetti, he designed it that way! In the beginning of this book, we referred to Adam and Eve. God is able to connect you two in marriage because it was he who instituted marriage in the garden long ago. Though you are not the first couple who ever lived, he cares about you and your future together just as if you were, and he has a plan for you that will take you beyond your wildest dreams.

News for the Newly Married

Dear Tech Support:

Recently I upgraded from Boyfriend 5.0 to Husband 1.0 and noticed that the new program began making unexpected changes to the accounting software, severely limiting access to wardrobe, flower, and jewelry applications that operated flawlessly under Boyfriend 5.0. No mention of this phenomenon was included in the product brochure. In addition, Husband 1.0 uninstalls many other valuable programs such as DinnerDancing 7.5, CruiseShip 2.3, and OperaNight 6.1 and installs new, undesirable programs such as PokerNight 1.3, SaturdayFootball 5.0, Golf 2.4, and ClutterEverywhere 4.5. Conversation 8.0 no longer runs and invariably crashes the system. Under no circumstances will it run DiaperChanging 14.1 or HouseCleaning 2.6. I've tried running Nagging 5.3 to fix Husband 1.0, but this all-purpose utility is of only limited effectiveness.

Can you help, please!!
Sincerely, XXX

Dear XXX:

This is a very common problem women complain about, but it is mostly due to a primary misconception. Many people upgrade from Boyfriend 5.0 to Husband 1.0 with no idea that Boyfriend 5.0 is merely an ENTERTAINMENT package. However, Husband 1.0 is an OPERATING SYSTEM and was designed by its creator to run as few applications as possible. Further, you cannot purge Husband 1.0 and return to Boyfriend 5.0, because Husband 1.0 is not designed to do this. Hidden operating files within your system would cause Boyfriend 5.0 to emulate Husband 1.0, so nothing is gained. It is impossible to uninstall, delete, or purge the program files from the system, once installed. Any new program files can only be installed once per year, as Husband 1.0 has severely limited memory. Error messages are common, and a normal part of Husband 1.0.

Having Husband 1.0 installed myself, I might also suggest you read the entire section regarding General Partnership Faults [GPFs]. This is a wonderful feature of Husband 1.0, secretly installed by the parent company as an integral part of the operating system. Husband 1.0 must assume ALL responsibility for ALL faults and problems, regardless of root cause. To activate this great feature enter the command "C:I THOUGHT YOU LOVED ME." Sometimes Tears 6.2 must be run simultaneously while entering the command. Husband 1.0 should then run the applications Apologize 12.3 and Flowers/Chocolates 7.8.

TECH TIP!

Avoid excessive use of this feature. Overuse can create additional and more serious GPFs, and ultimately YOU may have to give a C:IAPOLOGIZE command before the system will return to normal operations. Overuse can also cause Husband 1.0 to default to GrumpySilence 2.5, or worse yet, to Beer 6.0. Beer 6.0 is a very bad program that causes Husband 1.0 to create FatBelly files and SnoringLoudly wave files that are very hard to delete. Save yourself some trouble by following this tech tip!

Just remember, the system will run smoothly, and take the blame for all GPFs, but because of this fine feature it can only intermittently run all the applications Boyfriend 5.0 ran. Husband 1.0 is a great program, but it does have limited memory and cannot learn new applications quickly. Consider buying additional software to improve performance. I personally recommend HotFood 3.0, Lingerie 5.3, and Patience 10.1. Used in conjunction, these utilities can really help keep Husband 1.0 running smoothly.

After several years of use, Husband 1.0 will become familiar and you will find many valuable embedded features such as FixBrokenThings 2.1, Snuggling 4.2, and BestFriend 7.6. A final word of caution! DO NOT, under any circumstances, install MotherinLaw 1.0. This is not a supported application and will cause selective shutdown of the operating system. Husband 1.0 will run only Fishing 9.4 and Hunting 5.2 until MotherinLaw 1.0 is uninstalled. I hope these notes have helped. Thank you for choosing to install Husband 1.0, and we here at Tech Support wish you luck.[2]

Epilogue

The Secret Ingredient

The secret ingredient is always that special something that makes the food taste so good—so out of the ordinary. When people sense that there's something special in a recipe, they probe a little further and ask, "Hey, what's in this?" Bill and I have been asked that question for over 21 years. People have asked us how we stay in love, how our love stays fresh and strong. People ask us for the secret ingredient all the time.

That special something in our relationship is simply the grace and strength we each receive from our relationship with God. This ingredient really isn't too secret because he *wants* us to know him and the plan he has for our lives as husband and wife. But how can you tap into God's strength? How can you receive his grace for your own life, and for the marriage you desire to have? Read the statement below and simply, in prayer, receive his gift of love for you.

God's Statement of Love to Us

I love you and have a plan for you.

"I came to give life—life in all its fullness" (John 10:10).

"I came so they can have real and eternal life, more and better life than they ever dreamed of" (John 10:10 THE MESSAGE).

"God loved the world so much that he gave his one and only Son so that whoever believes in him may not be lost, but have eternal life" (John 3:16).

I know you are imperfect, so you are separated from my love. Our relationship is broken.

"All have sinned and are not good enough for God's glory" (Romans 3:23).

"We've compiled this long and sorry record as sinners...and proved that we are utterly incapable of living the glorious lives God wills for us..." (Romans 3:23 THE MESSAGE).

"Anyone who knows the right thing to do, but does not do it, is sinning" (James 4:17).

"It is your evil that has separated you from your God. Your sins cause him to turn away from you..." (Isaiah 59:2).

I love you, so I, who am perfect, paid the price for your imperfection so I could restore our relationship.

"But God shows his great love for us in this way: Christ died for us while we were still sinners. So through Christ we will surely be saved from God's anger, because we have been made right with God by the blood of Christ's death. While we were God's enemies, he made friends with us through the death of his Son. Surely, now that we are his friends, he will save us through his Son's life" (Romans 5:8-10).

"Christ had no sin, but God made him become sin so that in Christ we could become right with God" (2 Corinthians 5:21).

"Christ himself suffered for sins once. He was not guilty, but he suffered for those who are guilty to bring you to God" (1 Peter 3:18).

"The greatest love a person can show is to die for his friends" (John 15:13).

To initiate this new relationship, all you need to do is to accept my payment for your imperfection. I cannot make you love me, that is your choice.

"I mean that you have been saved by grace through believing. You did not save yourselves; it was a gift from God. It was not the result of your own efforts, so you cannot brag about it. God has made us what we are..." (Ephesians 2:8-10).

"If you use your mouth to say, 'Jesus is Lord,' and if you believe in your heart that God raised Jesus from the dead, you will be saved" (Romans 10:9).

"And this is eternal life: that people can know you, the only true God, and that they know Jesus Christ, the One you sent" (John 17:3).

To accept God's love for you, talk to him and tell him you want to let him lead the decision-making part of your life. This is a sample prayer:

Jesus, I am sorry I have chosen to live apart from you. I want you in my life. I accept the payment of love you gave for me by your death on the cross. Thank you for being my best friend and my God.

Bill and I have seen in our own life, and in the lives of countless other marriages, that the source and strength to love springs from the love God first gives us. We sign all of our books with the same verse that was etched into the wedding gifts we gave each other: *We love because he first loved us* (1 John 4:19).

Research indicates that those couples who have a strong relationship with God are more satisfied in their marriages and give their intimate, sexual lives the highest rating. Also, those couples who have friends who also believe in lifelong commitment in marriage tend to have longtime love—and happiness. Those who attend church regularly and are involved in serving rate their marriages as stronger and more satisfying emotionally, socially, and sexually.

Ecclesiastes 4:12 explains this source of strength: "Though one may be overpowered, two can defend themselves. A cord of three strands is not quickly broken." The three strands of you, your spouse, and God are an unbreakable team. As long as you keep God in the equation and seek to know him and obey him, your marriage will be fun and fulfilling. After all, it was God who created marriage way back in Eden.

Discussion Questions

These questions can be used for a couple to have a weekly Bible study together or for a small group to discuss and thus strengthen each other's marriages. We have found that couples who have a strong support network of friends who believe in long-term happy marriages tend to have long-lasting, happier marriages! These can also be used in conjunction with the *Men Are like Waffles—Women Are like Spaghetti* video series (see back page for ordering information).

Basics for good discussion groups:

Be personal. Greet each couple as they come. Try to provide an icebreaker question (the answers to these can be written on their name tags to enhance dialogue). A few icebreaker questions can include:

- Where did you go on your honeymoon?

- How old were you when you married?

- What's your favorite romantic spot in our area?

- Where was your wedding?

- What's one nice surprise you have gained as a married person?

Be early. Have the room set up for easy conversation: simple drinks (coffee, tea, water) and food are nice, chairs in a circle, etc. Romantic décor (fresh flowers, candlelight, and romantic music) is a nice addition.

Be prompt. Begin and end on time as childcare is often an issue. Feel free to end the meeting, but allow couples who want to stay to do so.

Be available. You may be needed between sessions for quick questions, prayer, and encouragement.

Be a leader. Don't put anyone on the spot, but try to keep everyone involved. You may need to say things like, "That was a great response, anyone else have any input?" Then look at the more reserved people eye to eye. To handle someone who dominates the group, you can say, "Before Gary shares, does anyone else have an answer/idea?" Or simply don't look at the dominator until you have scanned the crowd for other answers and input. If the person is very dominating, pull him or her aside individually and privately and say something like, "Joe, you are so quick thinking and your input is very valuable, but because you are so confident, others who are more reserved may not be sharing as much. Could you do me a favor and help me draw them out? Maybe count to five in your head before responding, or if you sense another group member might have something to share, look their way. I sense you are a natural leader, so I could use your help on this." Most people feel complimented and will respond positively.

Be creative. Go on a fun group date to a theater or miniature golfing. Have a group picnic or end-of-series dinner party. Give door prizes, present funny awards, or host a game-show-like evening. Fun ideas will model creativity in marriage. Compliment couples for creativity.

Be spiritual. It is always appropriate to open and close a gathering in prayer. You can pray, or connect them with another couple to pray. Pray conversationally as a group or ask for a volunteer to pray.

Chapter 1: What's the Difference?

"Let us make man in our image, in our likeness…so God created man in his own image, in the image of God he created him; male and female he created them" (Genesis 1:26-27).

What are some apparent differences between the genders that you have noticed? How are men and women different:

- In the way they use their time?

- In the way they use their money?

- In the way they parent?

- In the way they approach their careers?

- In the way they want to use free time?

- In the way they approach God?

- In what ways did you relate to the analogy, men are like waffles, women are like spaghetti?

- What are the benefits you can see in God creating us male and female?

Chapter 2: Waffles and Spaghetti Communicating

What kind of words should we use when talking with one another? Read the verses below and see if you gain any wisdom in your vocabulary and use of words in your relationship:

Ephesians 4:29

1 Thessalonians 5:11

Ephesians 5:4

James 1:19

Brainstorm together on ways to handle your anger. What can you do when you want to say something that will make matters worse. How can you handle the frustration and not hurt your spouse? For example, a simple tool is the use of "I" statements rather than "you" statements, which are often full of generalizations and accusations. It is easier to hear, "Honey, when you are late, I am afraid. Sometimes I feel devalued when you come home later than you said and you haven't called," rather than "Where have you been? You are always late! Can't you pick up a phone? Is it too much to ask that you stop your busy, important activities and call your wife, or am I not important enough to call?"

Have people in the group share a time when a weakness of theirs was causing stress in their marriage and God provided an answer to address the need.

Chapter 3: Waffles and Spaghetti Relaxing

Between the Sabbaths and the celebrations God lined out, the nation of Israel had 120 days off a year! Rest is important to God. Read Genesis 2:2-3 and Exodus 20:11. What principle do you see? What is one thing you do or don't do that makes you relaxed? How do you feel after you can enjoy that?

Compliment your spouse for something he or she does that takes the pressure off you.

When relaxing, how do you balance the differences? How do you make time to relax in ways you each enjoy? Have you discovered something you can do together to rest and relax?

Chapter 4: Waffles and Spaghetti in Love

Romance is one of the many practical ways you can encourage your spouse. We are called in Hebrews 3:13 to "encourage one another daily, as long as it is called Today, so that none of you may be hardened by sin's deceitfulness." The word "encourage" is made up of two Greek words—*para*, which means "alongside" and *kaleo*, which means "to be called." The word literally means, "called alongside to help." When you encourage your spouse, you are committing yourself to be alongside to help in whatever way you can. Sometimes it means cheerleading, sometimes it means confronting, sometimes it means flirting, and sometimes it means romancing. The amazing thing about encouragement is that it is the primary work of the Holy Spirit. In John 14:16, Jesus pointed out to his disciples, "And I will ask the Father, and he will give you another Counselor to be with you forever…" The word "Counselor" in this verse is the Greek word *paraclete* or "one who is called alongside." The Holy Spirit is in our lives to encourage, and when you encourage your spouse with romance you are making it easier for the Holy Spirit to do his work.

Romance is like a muscle that is built with practice. What are a few ideas that you gained in the chapter that you would like to practice?

Romance is the study of the person you love. What romantic personality type are you? Which type is your spouse? What did you learn about how your spouse would like to be romanced?

Chapter 5: Waffles and Spaghetti in the Bedroom

We recommend that for this chapter that the men form a small group and the women form a small group. Questions provided below are for a group of waffles and a separate group of spaghetti!

Waffles:

In the chapter, several verses were noted that share God's view on what is permissible in marital sex. Take a look at those verses more closely and see what phrase in each verse provides a principle of what is okay in marital sex: Genesis 2:24; Hebrews 13:4.

Read 1 Corinthians 7:3-5 and Philippians 2:3-5. How often should a couple have sex according to the verses?

Read Proverbs 5:18-19.

In light of these verses, let's talk about what is pornography. How can we recognize when something is going to lessen our value or desire for our spouse? Read the verses below and come up with a set of guidelines so you will know when to change the channel, turn off the TV, walk away from a magazine, and so on.

- Matthew 5:8
- Psalm 101:3
- Psalm 119:37
- Psalm 141:8
- Philippians 4:8
- Romans 12:2

Pornography brings in outside influences and violates God's plan for intimacy. What are some smart boundaries or choices you can make to protect your marriage from the negative influences of pornography?

Because women are like spaghetti, share one idea that you did for your wife *outside* the bedroom that caused her to want to be intimate with you. Tell us about one time you did something *right* that helped prepare your wife's heart for intimacy.

Because women are like spaghetti, sometimes the best gift is the gift of words. Share one line, compliment, or gift of words that encouraged your wife. How were you her "mirror?" (Examples: When Pam comes into my office, she usually says, "It's just me!" I respond with, "No, it's especially you!" One friend of mine also leaves a love note each morning in his wife's coffee cup.)

Spaghetti:

In the chapter, several verses were noted that share God's view on what is permissible in marital sex. Take a look at those verses more closely and see what phrase in each verse provides a principle of what is okay in marital sex: Genesis 2:24 Hebrews 13:4.

Read 1 Corinthians 7:3-5 and Philippians 2:3-5. How often should a couple have sex according to the verses?

What roadblocks do you have emotionally or physically or in your schedule that might be robbing time away from your intimate life? What is one step you can take this week to address that roadblock and see if you can cause some change in that circumstance?

Men are visually stimulated. They are also excited when a woman is confident about her sexuality. Read Song of Songs 7:1-13 and see what ideas you might get from the picture of this wife's relationship with her "king." (Note: Many Bible commentators believe verses 1-9 are Solomon's verbal description of what he sees and appreciates of his wife's body as she dances before him, and the rest of the chapter is her expression of what she'd like to see happen as a result.) What can you do that would make you feel more confident about your body or more confident of your sexuality?

Reread Song of Songs 7:10-13. What is one way you can creatively let your spouse know you are interested in him?

Chapter 6: Waffles and Spaghetti in Conflict

What do these verses teach about God's priority in conflict?

Romans 12:18

Romans 14:19

1 Corinthians 14:33

2 Corinthians 13:11

Ephesians 4:3

And how does this come about according to the verses below?

Galatians 5:22-23

Colossians 3:15

1 Peter 3:10-12

Ephesians 5:21

Philippians 2:1-5

What does John 13:34-35 say will be the result if you have peace as a goal in the midst of conflict and you seek to use God's power through the Holy Spirit to attain that goal?

Create a Conflict Covenant. List rules to argue by below. For example, our Conflict Covenant contains:

- Never throw anything! (That is why we hold hands when we argue—can't throw anything if you are holding hands!)
- Never walk out unless you are afraid you will break the commitment not to throw anything.
- Never name call.
- Never bring up divorce.

As a group, brainstorm rules for a fair fight that should be in a Conflict Covenant. Write your covenant and bring it back the following week and read it to the group.

Chapter 7: Waffles and Spaghetti Achieving Together

Sometimes we feel bad if we want to achieve for ourselves or our marriage or family. Read the verses below and give a synopsis of what you think God's view of achievement might be:

Ephesians 6:6-8

Philippians 3:14

1 Thessalonians 4:11-12

1 Corinthians 9:24

2 Timothy 4:7

Hebrews 12:1

How can you balance a heart set on achieving with God's clear care for "the least of these" and his model of a servant in the verses below?

John 13:3-5

Mark 9:35

James 4:10

1 Peter 5:6

What are some goals that you have:

• For yourself?

• For your marriage?

• For your home and family?

• For your career and ministry?

• That you'd like to see happen in the next five years?

Chapter 8: Waffles and Spaghetti at Home

When dividing tasks at home, it isn't who does *what* that is as important as the *attitude* with which you do it and the motivation behind the work. Read the verses below and find the common thread of motivation:

Matthew 25:23

Mark 9:35

Galatians 1:10

Galatians 5:13

Ephesians 6:7

One way to check to see if you have a servant's heart is the way in which you respond when you are treated as a servant. When is it hardest for you to be a servant? Choose a phrase from the verses above that you can repeat to yourself when you feel anger or resentment coming. For example, one of my (Pam's) favorite is "Whom am I trying to please? My goal is to please God."

What are things married partners can do to encourage and show appreciation for their spouse being a servant to the family? (Examples: Point out service to kids. "Hey, isn't Dad great for fixing the car?" Thank a spouse for daily duties. "Honey, that was a super dinner! Let me and the kids get the dishes."

Chapter 9: Waffles and Spaghetti As Parents

How is it helpful to have both a waffle and spaghetti as parents in a family?

What are the challenges for a man in parenting?

For a woman?

Think about each of your children. What area do they need to work on improving this next year? Which parent is better suited to meet that need? (For example, when the boys needed to learn to express themselves, I (Pam) helped them gain an adequate vocabulary. When they need to learn to follow through and stay on task, Bill is a better monitor.)

Waffles:

Consider this verse: Ephesians 6:4.

In what ways might you be exasperating your children?

Spaghetti:

1 Thessalonians 2:6-8 gives a word picture of the care the apostles showed those in Thessalonica. What wisdom do you see in what is said about the role of mom from these verses?

Ephesians 6:2-3 says: "'Honor your father and mother'—which is the first commandment with a promise—'that it may go well with you and that you may enjoy long life on the earth.'" How can you teach your children to appreciate the differences between genders? What is one way you can help them express appreciation to your spouse this week?

Chapter 10: Waffles and Spaghetti Meeting Each Other's Key Needs

If we have an accurate view of God, it can often help address our need for security and simplicity. Below is a short list of attributes of God. Think of which questions of security or simplicity is foremost on your heart and mind. What character trait of God's do you think might help meet that need in your life?

God is:

Father	Friend	All-knowing	All-powerful
A Refuge	A Shelter	A Sanctuary	A Shield
Victorious	King	Most High	Almighty
Gracious	Hope	Love	Joy
Peace	Patient	Kind	Good
Gentle	Helper	Redeemer	Light
Savior	Comforter	Healer	Faithful
True	Bridegroom	Holy	Just

These are just a few. Write down an area of your own personal weakness that you think has a negative impact on your relationship. What strength of God's could you draw on to fortify that area? For example, if I (Pam) am overly angry at the slightest offense, most likely the issue is more about me and the hurts I carry than about my spouse. So as I struggle with anger, I can look to God my PEACE for help and comfort. By learning all about the peace of God, I can gain clarity and a plan of how to better deal with my anger. By memorizing verses about peace, I have a new tape to play in my head when I sense the old tape of anger is about to go off!

Read the verses below. What encouragement do they give that can help you address the security and simplicity needs in your life?

2 Corinthians 3:5

2 Corinthians 12:9-10

If you can, share an area of weakness that you'd like the group to pray about for you. If anyone in the group has a verse about God's ability to give strength for that area, then have them either read the verse to you or write it down. You can take it home and memorize it, or use it as a springboard to cross-reference it and find other verses to help in your Bible.

Couple Communication Questions

Take these questions out on a date and discuss them over dinner or coffee. It is our hope these easy-to-use exercises will boost your appreciation of one another, deepen the intimacy of your marriage, and help make the differences of being a waffle and a spaghetti work *for* your relationship. It may help to copy these questions so you can each have a set, one for the waffle and one for the spaghetti. Then carry them with you to be ready for those key communication times, like in the car as you travel.

Chapter 1: What's the Difference?

Waffles:

What boxes do you feel successful in? Check the list below and mark the top three boxes you feel great about. Have your wife check the boxes she thinks you are successful at and discuss your answers.

__ Romance

__ Sex

__ Building/fixing home

__ Car

__ Fatherhood

__ Socializing

__ Working

__ Church/growing with God

__ Community involvement (coaching, clubs, etc.)

__ Political involvement

__ Investment/finance

__ Technical (computers, VCR, stereo and other electronic gadgets)

__ Educational/learning/schooling

__ Play (recreation, camping, hobbies, etc.)

Now which three do you feel less competent in—or even want to avoid!? Have your wife comment on the ones she feels you struggle with the most.

If you could be a woman for one day, what would you see as a positive opportunity?

Spaghetti:

Women are great at multitasking. Which tasks do you do on a daily/weekly basis that seem effortless to you, those you feel you can do with ease?

Have your husband discuss with you the tasks he is glad you handle. Which things does he think you do effortlessly as he watches you do them?

If you could be a man for just one day, what positive opportunity would you look forward to?

Chapter 2: Waffles and Spaghetti Communicating

Choose one of the three communication exercises below and go out to coffee and practice listening.

1. Each choose your favorite topic of conversation. Choose one person to be the listener and the other the communicator. The listener's job is to repeat key phrases and repeat back information for clarification in order to keep the other person talking for 15 minutes straight, then switch places.

2. Choose a topic that has been difficult to discuss in the past (kids, money, etc.). Each of you try to complete the statement below while the other uses repeating key phrases to try to move the conversation to a deeper level.

When I think of discussing _____ I feel _____ . (See list of words on next page.)

angry	exhausted	frustrated	threatened	guilty
confused	lonely	ashamed	depressed	overwhelmed
jealous	bored	anxious	reserved	depressed
stressed	used	attacked	irritated	sad
broken	squelched	trapped	fearful	betrayed
remorseful	helpless			

Choose a positive memory in your marriage. Now use the words below and describe how that positive moment made you feel:

ecstatic	confident	happy	joyful	hopeful
lovestruck	loved	inspired	peaceful	energized
proud	excited	complete	creative	relaxed
calm				

3. Now try to find a common denominator. When your spouse shares a feeling, ask him or her whether it feels like_____. Share a word picture or story of a time you think you might have had a similar feeling. Remember, don't be discouraged if it doesn't match up—you are talking and listening for discovery.

Chapter 3: Waffles and Spaghetti Relaxing

Waffles:

What are your three favorite boxes to go to for relaxing?

Spaghetti:

Who are three people you like to talk to when life becomes stressful?

For Both:

Is there an activity that you both enjoy that helps your husband relax and allows your wife to talk through her stress? Below are a few examples:

> Bowling
>
> Fishing
>
> Kayaking
>
> Boating
>
> Golfing
>
> Hunting
>
> Home improvement
>
> Get a massage
>
> Go on a walk

Make a date this next week to *do* a de-stressing activity together.

Chapter 4: Waffles and Spaghetti in Love

Each of you choose which romance personality from this chapter you think best describes you. Complete the worksheet below, trade romance worksheets, and each of you plan a date to please the other person! Put these dates on the calendar in *pen!*

My romance personality is:

10 free things that express love to me are:

> 1.

> 2.

> 3.

4.

5.

6.

7.

8.

9.

10.

10 dream dates I'd like to go on:

1.

2.

3.

4.

5.

6.

7.

8.

9.

10.

Size me up:

Shirt size   Shirt size

Pant size   Dress size

Shoe size   Shoe size

Favorite stores, restaurants, or other romantic resources with addresses, phone/websites

1.

2.

3.

4.

5.

Chapter 5: Waffles and Spaghetti in the Bedroom

The best commentary on what is acceptable and healthy in a sexual relationship in marriage is each other. Interview one another using the questions below to see what you love and what you'd like in your intimate life together:

• One thing I really love about our sex life is:

• I really love it when you:

• One thing I would love to try is:

• One boundary that we could agree on that might protect our marriage is:

Plan a 24-hour great escape. Where will you go? What will you do? Who will arrange travel? Child care? Financing? Delegate and dream together. Put the date on the calendar. One pastor friend of ours gave some wise advice to a new colleague, just out of seminary: *Whisk your wife away for 24 hours once a month to a hotel and you will have the energy and motivation to stay in love and stay in ministry!* Invest in your intimate life, and your relationship will have what it takes to weather the storm. Another couple made a commitment to put $1 in the bank each time they made love, to save for a second honeymoon. Some days he'd come in the house and say, "Got a dollar!" and she would respond, "I know how to spend it!" This tradition sent them to all the best places in Hawaii for their 50th anniversary. When he got home, he turned to her and said, "I think we should save for a trip to Cancun…got a dollar!"

Each of you think of an idea to weave intimacy into your routine. Share the ideas with one another. You may consider our tradition of kissing after each time we pray together. Or, you may want to kiss each time you greet or leave one another. Make it simple and it will stick. Do you have a dollar?

Chapter 6: Waffles and Spaghetti in Conflict

For this chapter, we recommend a day away, or a weekend away together, so you have ample, uninterrupted time to talk through issues that may be keeping you apart or causing stress in your relationship. If time away doesn't help enough, we encourage you to value your relationship and make an appointment with a pastor or qualified Christian marriage counselor. How you handle conflict is a vital indication of your ability to maintain a long-lasting, satisfying relationship together. Read through this section ahead of the time away. You might want to make preparations for your time together.

Think of a phrase you can use to cut the hot lead. For example, "If we keep discussing this in raised voices, I may get my feelings hurt," or "Please don't call me names, I will respond better if you will just share your heart."

Password worksheet:
List three things that attracted you to your spouse

    1.

    2.

    3.

Now answer these questions to help give you some ideas on what to use for a password:

What are a few of your favorite romantic memories?

What is a joke you two share? Or something that makes you laugh together?

Do you have a favorite TV show or commercial you both enjoy?

Brainstorm two to three ideas of what passwords might work in your relationship:

Forgiveness Exercise. Turn to the forgiveness section in this chapter. Choose one stress, frustration, betrayal, or irritation you can and will forgive your spouse for. Silently pray through the steps of forgiveness.

Now make a list of "things I think I need forgiveness for" and share those things with your spouse. If he or she is ready, they can choose to pray the steps of forgiveness over those issues—but don't force them or be disappointed if they are not ready yet. Sometimes the offended party needs time to process the hurt before he or she can release and forgive.

You may choose to use this as a time of recommitment. Below are a few ideas of expressions of recommitment:

- Renew your vows. This can be done by a pastor in front of loved ones, or privately at the foot of your bed, or at a favorite romantic setting.

- Return to a first love. Visit a place you first kissed, first said I love you, proposed—and do it all over again.

- Give a symbolic gift. Make a photo frame, album, shadow box of wedding pictures, momentos, or favorite marriage memories. Or give the gift of releasing a spouse from something you've held against them. Tie it to a balloon and release it, burn a list in the fireplace, or take a hike to a retreat center and place it at the foot of a mountain cross.

- Buy and exchange new rings. One couple purchased rings that showed their first commitment was to God, and that in God they can find the forgiveness and grace to go forward in their marriage. They wear these on their wedding band finger—of the opposite hand.

Chapter 7: Waffles and Spaghetti Achieving Together

Complete the exercises below and share your reponses:

Some hopes and dreams I have for the next five years are:

One way I would sense your applause and approval is if you would:

Research indicates that men take greater risks. How do you feel about the way your spouse handles risk?

Research also says men tend to be overconfident and women underconfident. What area in your life do you think you are good at but might not give yourself credit for?

Life is full of natural transitions. What is coming in the next three to five years in your family life and marriage that you should anticipate, prepare, and plan for?

Here are some of my ideas that might help address those issues:

Chapter 8: Waffles and Spaghetti at Home

Write each of the following "Life Responsibilities" on 3 x 5 cards. You will each need a set. Rank each item with a 1, 2, or 3. A 1 means it is very important to you. You would keep your 1 activities even if you never could do a 2 or 3. A 2 means it is important, though not a main focus, but you don't feel like it can go undone. A 3 means if it gets done fine, but if it doesn't, no sweat. The 3s are those things that can drop out of life when things get hectic or the quality can suffer a bit and it doesn't make you crazy.

Life Responsibilities

____ Being in good physical shape

____ Having a neat, clean home

____ Having your family finances in order

____ Maintaining correspondence

____ Having quality intimacy/romance

____ Having time with your children (like overseeing home-work, team parent, etc.)

____ Having fun as a family (like trips, vacations, kick around time)

____ Succeeding in your career

____ Having a personal ministry/involvement in church

___ Extracurricular activities (like community involvement, career enhancement, philanthropic activities)

___ Having a nice car(s)

___ Furthering your education

___ Achieving more financial success

___ Time alone

___ Time with God

___ Time with mate (talking, relating nonsexually)

___ Time for a hobby

___ Other_____

Now compare your cards. Which things are ranked the same? Mark those with a *. You're probably less likely to argue over those areas. Circle the areas that have the greatest differences. (Like yours is a 1 and his is a 3!) You'll have to negotiate in these areas. They are hot spots.

Set a date to negotiate these responsibilities with each other. Keep in mind you two don't have to *do* all those responsibilities. This is a great time to delegate to household help, like to a housekeeper, or to enlist the children so they grow into responsible adults. Each of you will need to *oversee* key areas of responsibility: the care and maintenance of the home, finances, children, cars, etc.

Chapter 9: Waffles and Spaghetti As Parents

Waffle and Spaghetti Together

List your kids along with their strengths and weaknesses. Then decide which of you (the waffle or spaghetti) might need to set aside time to build up an area of weakness.

-

-

-

-

-

Compliment your spouse in an area of parenting where being spaghetti /a waffle is valuable.

For example: *Your ability to multitask is helping the boys to balance all their responsibilities well. You've done a great job getting them student planners and calendars and helping them use them.*

Or: *Your ability to stay in one box was really great when Brock was having to learn how to take care of his new car and he had to fix the brakes. There were so many people in and out that day and so many wanted to interrupt, but you made Brock a priority—thanks!*

Chapter 10: Waffles and Spaghetti Meeting Each Other's Key Needs

Men, are you asking any of these questions?

1. Is life with you going to be filled with admiration?

2. Is life with you going to be free from complications?

3. Is life with you going to be sexual?

4. Is life with you going to be cooperative?

5. Is life with you going to be lived in the present?

Women, are you asking any of these questions?

1. Am I more important than our money?

2. Are you being sincere?

3. Do you notice me?

4. Am I more important than your sleep?

5. Do you notice other women?

Choose one from each list for discussion. Ask each other, "When you ask this question, what response would you like to receive from me?"

For example, when Pam gets a new outfit or haircut, she likes me to notice. So I now put "Notice Pam's hair" in my Palm Pilot the day she has a hair appointment. Or if she goes shopping, I note it in my Palm Pilot. Pam has agreed to give me the heads up on these things when we meet for our calendar date once a week. She is setting me up for success rather than failure.

Or when Bill is needing extra admiration, he will begin a conversation with an obvious statement, such as, "I did good on this, didn't I?" or "Pam, come look at what I just finished and admire it with me." By giving obvious clues, I can respond successfully.

Research indicates that those couples who have a strong relationship with God are more satisfied in their marriages and give their intimate, sexual lives the highest rating. Over dinner, or on a walk, talk about what spiritual activity from the list below would build your relationship at this time. Try to communicate why that activity is valuable to you and how you feel when you do it.

• Attend a church worship service together weekly.

• Have a daily devotional time together. (Try *Quiet Times for Couples* by Norm Wright.)

• Have individual devotional times daily, then discuss over coffee, or on a walk, what God is teaching each of you.

• Pray together over meals and/or at bedtime each evening.

• Attend a Sunday school class or small-group Bible study together.

- Lead a couples' Bible study. (Be the facilitators of a *Men Are like Waffles—Women Are like Spaghetti* video discussion group for couples.)

- Volunteer together. Teach a children's Sunday school or Awana class. Be youth group sponsors or chaperones.

- Pray a blessing over each other. Try to do it daily. It can be as simple as walking through the kitchen and placing your hand on a shoulder and whispering in her ear, "God, thanks for a great-looking wife!" Or when the bathroom mirror is steamed up, etch in the fog, "God, thanks for a great guy!"

Or it may be longer such as, "God, thank you for this woman who seems to be able to multitask with ease. Thank you that she has the ability to keep the details of life and our family in order and in motion. Thank you for her creativity and encouragement. I feel so fortunate to have her as my wife." Or "God, thanks so much for my husband. I don't know what I would do without him. He rescues me so often because you have given him the ability to stay in a box and fix problems long after the feelings for the task are gone. Thank you for his diligence and his wonderful listening ear. Lord, please bless him because he is such a blessing to me."

Notes

Chapter 1

1. Daniel J. Canary and Tara M. Emmers-Sommner with Sandra Faulkner, *Sex and Gender Differences in Personal Relationships* (New York, NY: The Guilford Press, 1997), p. v.
2. Contributed by Darleen Giannini, *Reader's Digest*, April 1995, Vol. 146, No. 876, p. 85.
3. Contributed by Gary L. Webb, *Reader's Digest*, April 1995, Vol. 146, No. 876, p. 130.
4. Contributed by Robert Ford, *Readers Digest*, April 1995, Vol. 146, No. 876, p. 130.
5. Leah Ariniello, *Gender and the Brain* (Washington, D.C.: Society for Neuroscience, 1998, via ProQuest, an information service by Bell & Howell).
6. Ibid.
7. Ibid.
8. Malcolm Ritter, *Brains Differ in Navigation Skills*, AP Science Writer, Tuesday, March 21, 2000.
9. Ibid.
10. Ariniello.
11. "Aggressive Driving Analyzed: The Effect of Age, Gender, and Type of Car Driven Across the States" ©1999 by Dr. Leon James (DrDriving). Found at www.DrDriving.com.
12. Bernice Kanner, *Are You a Normal Guy?* American Demographics, Ithaca, March 1999, Volume 21, Issue 3, p. 19. Obtained via ProQuest, a Bell & Howell information service.
13. Nancy Ammon Jianakoplos and Alexandra Bernasek, *Are Women More Risk Averse?* Economic Inquiry, Huntington Beach, Oct 1998, Volume 36, Issue 4, pp. 620-630. Obtained via ProQuest, a Bell & Howell information service.
14. Sheila Brownlow, Rebecca Whitener, and Janet M. Rupert, "'I'll Take Gender Differences for $1000!' Domain-Specific Intellectual: Success on *Jeopardy*," *Sex Roles* (New York, Feb. 1998). Obtained via ProQuest, a Bell & Howell information service.
15. Ibid.
16. Ibid.
17. Jianakoplos, pp. 620-630.
18. Ibid.
19. Kanner, p. 19.
20. Ibid.
21. Lillian Glass, Ph.D., *He Says, She Says* (New York, NY: Berkley Publishing Group, Perigree Books, 1993) p. 33.
22. Ibid., p. 34.
23. Author Unknown.

Chapter 2

1. Clipping handed to us from a *Dear Abby* column, Dear Abby, P.O. Box 69440, Los Angeles, CA 90069.

Chapter 3

1. Ralph R. Behnke and Chris R. Sawyer, "Anticipatory Anxiety Patterns for Male and Female Public Speakers," *Communication Education*, (2000), Volume 49, Issue 2, pp. 187-195.
2. Ibid.
3. Ibid.
4. Canary, p. 31.
5. Dave and Claudia Arp, *The Ultimate Marriage Builder: A Do-It-Yourself Encounter Weekend for You and Your Mate* (Nashville, TN: Thomas Nelson, 1994), p. 19.
6. Author Unknown. *Homiletics*, January 2000, p. 18.

Chapter 4

1. For more on personalities: Florence Littauer, Marita Littauer, *Getting Along with Almost Anybody: The Complete Personality Book* (Ada, MI: Fleming H. Revell, 1998); Jim Brawner, Suzette Brawner, Gary Smalley, *Taming the Family Zoo: Maximizing Harmony and Minimizing Family Stress* (Colorado Springs, CO: NavPress, 1998); and Bob Phillips, *The Delicate Art of Dancing with Porcupines: Learning to Appreciate*

the Finer Points of Others (Ventura, CA: Regal Books, 1989).

Chapter 5
1. www.jokesplus.com.
2. John Nicholson, *Men and Women* (Oxford, England: Oxford University Press, 1984), p. 12.
3. Ibid., p. 39.
4. Simon LeVay, *The Sexual Brain* (Cambridge, MA: The MIT Press, 1993), p. 53.
5. Nicholson, p. 147.
6. Ibid., p. 144.
7. Ibid., pp. 144-5.
8. Ibid., p. 145.
9. www.jokesplus.com.
10. Nicholson, pp. 141-2.
11. Author unknown.

Chapter 6
1. Canary, p. 82.
2. Ibid.
3. Ibid.
4. Ibid.
5. Ibid., p. 34.
6. Lillian Glass, Ph.D., *He Says, She Says* (New York, NY: Perigree Books 1993), p. 131.

Chapter 7
1. www.jokesplus.com.
2. Associated Press, "Finally…Computer Games for Girls," *USA Today*, 02/03/99.
3. Ibid.
4. Ibid.
5. Ibid.
6. Ibid.
7. L.C. Embrey & J.J. Fox, "Gender Differences in the Investment Decision-Making Process," *Financial Counseling and Planning*, 8(2), (1997), pp. 33-40.
8. Ibid.
9. Susan Roxburgh, "Exploring the Work and Family Relationship," *Journal of Family Issues* (Beverly Hills, CA), Nov. 1999, Volume 20, Issue 6, pp. 771-788, obtained via ProQuest, a Bell & Howell information service.
10. Maria Gardiner and Marika Tiggemann, "Gender Differences in Leadership

Style, Job Stress and Mental Health in Male- and Female-Dominated Industries, *Journal of Occupational and Organizational Psychology*: Leicester, Sep. 1999, Volume 72, Part 3, pp. 301-315. Obtained via ProQuest, a Bell & Howell information service.
11. Kaia Rendahl, Jean Anderson, Kristin Hill, Anna Henning, Christopher Randall, Amy Davis, Psychology Group at St. Olaf University, results of survey.
12. Ahalya Krishnan, Christopher J. Sweeney, "Gender Differences in Fear of Success Imagery and Other Achievement-Related Background Variables Among Medical Students," *Sex Roles*, August 1998, Volume 39; Issue 3,4, pp. 299-310. Obtained via ProQuest, a Bell & Howell information service.
13. Ibid.
14. Gardiner, pp. 301-315.
15. Ibid.
16. Ibid.
17. Ibid.
18. Roxburgh, pp. 771-88.
19. Ibid.
20. Ibid.
21. Patrick Morley, *The Man in the Mirror* (Brentwood, TN: Wolgemuth & Hyatt Publishers, Inc., 1989), p. 84.
22. Author Unknown.

Chapter 8
1. www.preachingtoday.com
2. Canary, p. 106.
3. Ibid., pp. 105-06.
4. Ibid., p. 110.
5. Ibid., p. 111.
6. Ibid., p. 112.
7. Canary, Daniel J., Tara M. Emmers-Sommer with Sandra Faulkner, *Sex and Gender Differences in Personal Relationships* (New York, NY: The Guilford Press, 1997), p. 156. The authors point out that Agostinelli (1988) found that men reported that they do desire an equitable arrangement in the division of labor, but women reported that they simply wanted men to help them more with traditionally female chores (regardless of concerns for equitable

arrangements for the division of labor).

8. Nicholson, pp. 114-15.
9. Canary, p. 154.
10. Canary, Daniel J., Tara M. Emmers-Sommer with Sandra Faulkner, *Sex and Gender Differences in Personal Relationships* (New York, NY: The Guilford Press, 1997), p. 109. They quote researchers—South and Spitze (1994) reported that women spend an average of 32.6 hours per week on housework, whereas men spend only 18.1 hours per week on chores. South and Spitze noted that these figures reverse when examining paid employment; that is, men work an average of 32 hours a week in paid jobs, whereas women work an average of about 18 hours a week in paid jobs. According to these figures, men and women appear to be working virtually the same amount of time. Similarly, Ferree (1991) found that both husbands and wives reported that they and their partners work about 60 hours per week (with men engaged in longer hours at paid jobs). Ferree concluded, "Because wives do about 10 hours less of paid work and 10 hours more of housework, the overall average difference in workload (exclusive of child care) is trivial" (p. 72).

Chapter 9

1. Nicholson, p. 131.
2. Ibid., p. 129.
3. Ibid.
4. Ibid., p. 131.
5. Ibid.
6. Ibid.
7. Ibid., p. 128.
8. Brenda Hunter, *Where Have All the Mothers Gone* (Grand Rapids, MI: Zondervan, 1982), p. 88.
9. Ibid.
10. Ibid., p. 89.
11. Nicholson, p. 124.
12. Ibid.
13. Hunter, p. 93.

Chapter 10

1. Canary, p. 13.
2. Author unkown.

For more resources to enhance your relationships and build marriages or to connect with Pam and Bill Farrel for a speaking engagement, contact:

Farrel Communications
Masterful Living
PO Box 1507
San Marcos, CA 92079
(800) 810-4449

http://farrelcommunications.com
www.Masterfulliving.com

Be sure to ask about
Men Are like Waffles—Women Are like Spaghetti
Video Series

Great for individual couples or groups!

More Bill and Pam Farrel Books from Harvest House Publishers

MEN ARE LIKE WAFFLES—WOMEN ARE LIKE SPAGHETTI STUDY GUIDE
Bill and Pam Farrel

Go to a new level in your appreciation of the differences and special delights of your mate! Designed to address the important issues of a happy marriage, this guide will

- make planning time with each other fun and exciting
- help you and your mate coordinate parenting so your kids get the best
- bring out the best you have to give in sex, romance, and communication

This study is great for leading couples in biblically based discussions or for couples to use on their own to create their own marriage retreat.

SINGLE MEN ARE LIKE WAFFLES—SINGLE WOMEN ARE LIKE SPAGHETTI
Bill and Pam Farrel

Do you wonder how to relate to the opposite sex? Do you want to build a stronger relationship with your girlfriend or boyfriend? In this great book, Bill and Pam help "waffles" and "spaghettis" explore:

- how to meet other singles
- the advantages and disadvantages of being male and female
- what to do if you're single again with kids

Discover how a relationship with God can fulfill your key needs. A discussion guide is included for small group or personal use.

RED-HOT MONOGAMY: MAKING YOUR MARRIAGE SIZZLE
Bill and Pam Farrel

Did you know that the best sexual experiences are enjoyed by married couples? Bill and Pam reveal how to add spark and sizzle to your love life. Discover how

- God specifically designed you to give and receive pleasure from your mate
- a little skill turns marriage into red-hot monogamy
- sex works best emotionally, physically, and physiologically

Along with ways to create intimacy when you're just too tired and how to avoid "pleasure thieves," this book offers hundreds of ideas to inspire romance and passion.

10 Best Decisions a Couple Can Make
Bill and Pam Farrel

Bestselling authors and popular speakers Bill and Pam Farrel provide readers with a tool chest of communication skills for do-it-yourselfers who want to get the most out of their marriage. HGTV watchers and *Better Homes and Gardens* readers will quickly connect with the home-improvement theme as the Farrels show couples how to...

- strengthen the foundation of their family
- inspect their marriage for hidden weak spots
- protect their relational investment with consistent maintenance and improvement

Filled with practical advice, biblical insights, and the Farrel's trademark warmth and wit, this manual is perfect for newlyweds as well as longtime marriage partners as they turn their fixer-upper marriage into the relationship of their dreams.

The 10 Best Decisions Every Parent Can Make
Bill and Pam Farrel

With three active children, Bill and Pam know what they're talking about in this book filled with wisdom and encouragement. The Farrels offer specific ideas for nurturing your children, including prodigals and those with special needs or strong-wills.

Packed with creative, motivational tools and games that allow children to blossom and succeed. Help your children become everything God designed them to be.

The 10 Best Decisions a Woman Can Make
Pam Farrel

Pam encourages you to exchange the fleeting standards of the world for the steadfast truths found in a growing, fruitful relationship with God. You'll discover the joy of finding your place in God's plan as you

- realize how precious you are to the Lord
- find a positive place to direct your creativity, energy, and enthusiasm
- gain confidence regarding the value of your time and efforts

Pam's warm, motivating message will touch your heart as you seek all God has for you.